Emotional Literacy in the early years

by Sue Allingham

Contents

What is 'Emotional Literacy'?	2
Nurturing emotional literacy in the early years	8
How emotional literacy supports wellbeing	14
The role of the adult	20
Working in partnership with parents	26
How emotional literacy supports an inclusive environment	31
Emotional literacy in daily provision and the curriculum	34
Fostering emotional literacy in the setting	40
Appendices	47
• An audit of provision	
• The Emotional Health Lead	
• Key vocabulary of emotions	
References	54
Acknowledgements	56

Published by Practical Pre-School Books, A Division of MA Education Ltd, St Jude's Church, Dulwich Road, Herne Hill, London, SE24 0PB. Tel: 020 7738 5454 www.practicalpreschoolbooks.com

© MA Education Ltd 2020

Design: Mary Holmes fonthillcreative 01722 717036

All images © MA Education Ltd.

All rights reserved. No part of this publication may be reproduced, stored in a retrieval system, or transmitted by any means, electronic, mechanical, photocopied or otherwise, without the prior permission of the publisher.

ISBN 978-1-912611-20-1

What is 'Emotional Literacy'?

Play to man, especially in childhood, is a mirror both of thoughts and feelings, and of surroundings. In childhood it is emphatically a mirror of the innate need for life and occupation. (Froebel, 1897)

How are you in the world?

It is important to make clear from the outset that feeling positive socially and emotionally, and knowing that you are cared about and respected is crucial for all humans throughout their lives. From birth to seven years of age, is the key time to develop and underpin this security as the brain is developing.

> A complex range of factors have an impact on social and emotional development. Knowledge of these factors may help encourage investment at a population level in early interventions to support health and wellbeing. This would ensure children (and families) who are most likely to experience the poorest outcomes get the help they need early on in their lives. Knowledge of these factors, aside, practitioners' experience and expertise will be paramount in assessing the needs and risks of individual children and their families. (NICE 2012)

It is right and proper that there is a focus on children and families who may 'experience the poorest outcomes' – the word 'vulnerable' is often used – but the aim of this book is to unpick the social and emotional development for all involved in Early Childhood Education and how vital it is to promote 'emotional literacy'.

> Social and emotional wellbeing is important in its own right, but it also provides the basis for future health and life chances. (NICE 2012)

Chapter One: What is 'Emotional Literacy'?

Each chapter of this book will contain case studies to prompt discussion and encourage reflection. These have been taken from my own experiences, or have been shared with me by colleagues and friends.

Getting it right from the start

Throughout this book the aim is to examine how we actually understand, reflect, underpin and support the variety of emotions shown daily in our settings by adults and children alike. What do we need to enable us to be 'emotionally literate' and encourage it in others?

We live in a world where there is an increasing recognition of emotional health and the impact it has on quality of life. We must view this recognition through two lenses, which will be referred to throughout the book:

- Our core documents, both statutory and for guidance, as they consistently remind us of this with references to personal, social and emotional development
- Our own feelings and understandings, as they will determine how we understand and interpret what we read.

Let's look at some examples from the statutory documents of the different countries of the United Kingdom.

> **Note**
>
> As you read, note down all the words that reflect **emotions**, **feelings**, **wellbeing** and **happiness**. Keep this list and refer to it as you read this book. You will find that you add more words and reflect on what they mean to you and those around you.

England

Statutory Framework for the Early Years Foundation Stage (EYFS 2017).

Although the word 'emotion' is mentioned only a handful of times, there is a constant thread of the welfare of the child underpinning the document. For example:

1. Every child deserves the best possible start in life and the support that enables them to fulfil their potential. Children develop quickly in the early years and a child's experiences between birth and age five have a major impact on their future life chances. A secure, safe and happy childhood is important in its own right. Good parenting and high quality early learning together provide the foundation children need to make the most of their abilities and talents as they grow up. (DFE 2017)

The Statutory Framework is built on four 'principles':

- every child is a unique child, who is constantly learning and can be resilient, capable, confident and self-assured
- children learn to be strong and independent through positive relationships
- children learn and develop well in enabling environments, in which their experiences respond to their individual needs and there is a strong partnership between practitioners and parents and/ or carers
- children develop and learn in different ways (see "the characteristics of effective teaching and learning" at paragraph 1.9) and at different rates. The framework covers the education and care of all children in early years provision, including children with special educational needs and disabilities. (DFE 2017)

These are demonstrated through Personal, Social and Emotional Development as an 'area of learning', which is given core importance as a 'Prime Area'.

> Personal, social and emotional development involves helping children to develop a positive sense of themselves, and others; to form positive relationships and develop respect for others; to develop social skills and learn how to manage their feelings; to understand appropriate behaviour in groups; and to have confidence in their own abilities (DFE 2017)

This core theme of personal, social and emotional development as a curriculum requirement is reflected in the key documents across the UK. This Statutory Framework also contains what is meant by the 'Characteristics of Effective Teaching and Learning' and how these must give shape to our work. We will be returning to the

Chapter One: What is 'Emotional Literacy'?

'Characteristics' in the final chapters of this book, as they are a component of an emotionally literate environment.

Northern Ireland

Learning to Learn - A Framework for Early Years Education and Learning.

Once again the importance of personal, social and emotional development is emphasised.

> The actions are aimed at ensuring that every child can access high quality early learning experiences that equip them to develop improved cognitive, social and emotional skills and which lay important foundations for future learning and development. (DENI 2013)

Early Years 1.1 A child's success in school and life is significantly determined at a very young age, and before they start school. Today we know more than ever about the importance of positive and supportive environments and their impact on brain development, and we understand more than ever how much the first years of a child's life can shape the rest of their life. (DENI 2013)

Policy Objectives 4.6 In support of the policy aim, the policy objectives are to: provide equitable access to high quality early years education and learning services; support personal, social and emotional development, promote positive learning dispositions and enhance language, cognitive and physical development in young children; (DENI 2013)

Wales

Foundation Phase Framework.

The Welsh Foundation Phase Framework is the statutory curriculum for all three to seven year olds in Wales.

> The Foundation Phase encompasses the developmental need of children. At the centre of the statutory curriculum lies the holistic development of children and their skills, building on their previous learning experiences and knowledge. The Foundation Phase curriculum promotes equality of opportunity and values, and celebrates diversity. Positive partnerships with the home are fostered and an appreciation of parents/carers being the children's first educators is recognised. (Welsh Government 2015)

The importance of emotional development and wellbeing must also be recognised. It should be acknowledged that children as young as 36 months are very much at the early stages of their development. The experiences that children have had before entering the setting/school need to be recognised and considered. It is essential that children have access to a variety of media to express themselves and ample opportunities to apply their imagination in a purposeful way.

Children acquire and develop skills at different rates and must be allowed to develop at their own unique, individual pace. As children learn new skills they should be given opportunities to practise them in different situations, to reflect on and evaluate their work. In all aspects of their development, children's own work should be respected, valued and encouraged for its originality and honesty. (Welsh Government 2015)

Chapter One: What is 'Emotional Literacy'?

We aim to ensure that all children and young people:

- have a flying start in life and the best possible basis for their future growth and development
- have access to a comprehensive range of education, training and learning opportunities, including acquisition of essential personal and social skills
- enjoy the best possible physical and mental, social and emotional health, including freedom from abuse, victimisation and exploitation
- have access to play, leisure, sporting and cultural activities
- are listened to, treated with respect, and are able to have their race and cultural identity recognised
- have a safe home and a community that supports physical and emotional wellbeing
- are not disadvantaged by any type of poverty.

Scotland

Curriculum for Excellence.

The document opens with a section on health and wellbeing. It is emphasised that:

> Children and young people should feel happy, safe, respected and included in the school environment and all staff should be proactive in promoting positive behaviour in the classroom, playground and the wider school community. Robust policies and practice which ensure the safety and wellbeing of children should already be in place.
>
> Every child has these rights, I (the child) can expect my learning environment to support me to:

- develop my self-awareness, self-worth and respect for others
- meet challenges, manage change and build relationships
- experience personal achievement and build my resilience and confidence
- understand and develop my physical, mental and spiritual wellbeing and social skills
- understand how what I eat, how active I am and how decisions I make about my behaviour and relationships affect my physical and mental wellbeing
- participate in a wide range of activities which promote a healthy lifestyle
- understand that adults in my school community have a responsibility to look after me, listen to my concerns and involve others where necessary
- earn about where to find help and resources to inform choices
- assess and manage risk and understand the impact of risk-taking behaviour
- reflect on my strengths and skills to help me make informed choices when planning my next steps
- acknowledge diversity and understand that it is everyone's responsibility to challenge discrimination.

Strong links are made between emotional wellbeing and learning across the whole curriculum.

United Nations Convention on the Rights of the Child

Having reflected on our national documents, it's important to remember that we must also consider the rights of the child. It is not always clear how national policy and guidance reflects these.

The UN Convention on the Rights of the Child 1989 states:

> **article 24 (health and health services)**. Every child has the right to the best possible health. Governments must provide good quality health care, clean water, nutritious food, and a clean environment and education on health and well-being so that children can stay healthy. Richer countries must help poorer countries achieve this.
>
> **article 29 (goals of education)**. Education must develop every child's personality, talents and abilities to the full. It must encourage the child's respect for human rights, as well as respect for their parents, their own and other cultures, and the environment.
>
> **article 31 (leisure, play and culture)**. Every child has the right to relax, play and take part in a wide range of cultural and artistic activities.

The final key document to consider here is one that affects England and Wales.

Chapter One: What is 'Emotional Literacy'?

Childcare Act 2006

In part one:

GENERAL FUNCTIONS OF LOCAL AUTHORITY, ENGLAND it states:

Improvement of young children's well-being

(2) In this Act "well-being", in relation to children, means their well-being so far as relating to
(a) physical and mental health and emotional well-being;
(b) protection from harm and neglect;
(c) education, training and recreation;

This range of references demonstrates how the importance of understanding emotional development included in the policy documents that we are given dictates, underpins and informs our practice in the United Kingdom. A search of policy in any country in the world will, however, demonstrate the same thinking.

Case studies and terminology

Having established our statutory position regarding working with emotional health, this first case study will enable you to start reflecting on what this means and looks like in practice. All case studies use the key vocabulary below.

Parent: for the purposes of this book the term 'parent' covers any adult who is acting in a parental role for the child.

Setting: this term is used to cover any environment that children attend away from their own home. This includes the home of a childminder, or a school.

Teacher: throughout this book the term 'teacher' is used to refer to all adults who work with young children and plan for their learning. In this way the term is used much more broadly than the definition of Qualified Teacher Status and covers the range of adults that children and their families will meet in each setting they access.

Key Person: Each child must be assigned a key person. Their role is to help ensure that every child's care is tailored to meet their individual needs (in accordance with paragraph 1.10), to help the child become familiar with the setting, offer a settled relationship for the child and build a relationship with their parents. (DfE 2017)

It is aim of this book to be used by teams as a discussion point. This means that everyone must be clear of their roles within the provision and that a consistent message is given to children and families alike.

Self-reflection is not always easy. The case studies can be used to open discussions in which all contributions are valuable.

Chapter One: What is 'Emotional Literacy'?

Case study: A little boy

It was Omar's first full session at Nursery. His Mother sat and watched him for a while, as the team had requested. The 'Settling in Policy' had been shared with her, and she had already brought her son for three short visits.

Omar had enjoyed his visits, and appears to have settled well. It was now time for him to be left for his first session without his Mother. She stands up to leave and her Key Person advises her to leave quickly before her son notices. However, she is carrying her new baby and he makes a little sound, as his Mother moves. Her older son notices and runs over to her as she makes her way to the door. He clings onto her leg crying. The Key Person comes across and gently removes the little boy from his Mother's leg. He remains very upset, but his Mother leaves. By now she is also upset and the baby is fractious.

Once the Mother has left, the Key Person kneels down beside the little boy and says,

'Don't worry, Mummy will come back. She has left her front door key with me, so she will have to come back for that won't she?' She produces a key from her pocket, it is a generic one and doesn't belong to the Mother.

This is a standard practice in the setting as part of their 'settling in' process, and has been recommended by an Adviser. The little boy takes the key and settles a little. However, he keeps checking the door, and will not let go of the key and cries intermittently. The Key Person is involved in a group activity as is no longer paying attention to him.

What do you notice here? What do you feel?

There are several emotions shown in this story. What are they and who shows them? What would you do?

Conclusion

As you began reading this chapter your task was to keep a list of all the words you noticed that related to emotions, feelings, or wellbeing. You may also be adding words that describe your feelings. Keep adding to this list and, as you read further, reflect on each word noted. What do they mean to you? Do they all mean the same? Can they be interpreted very differently? For example, is 'emotional literacy' the same as 'emotional intelligence'? I will return to this throughout the book.

Understanding the importance of nuance, and difference will become increasingly apparent throughout this book, in both the use of words and what we observe.

Think about...

You may have added these three words to your list:

- **Compassion**
- **Empathy**
- **Sympathy**.

They all relate to sharing emotion in some way, but do they all mean the same? Consider how the use of some words can have the potential to make the situation worse rather than better.

In the next chapter we will examine what is meant by 'emotional literacy' in more depth and what needs to considered as we move towards putting understanding into practice.

> Learning to manage one's emotions occurs over time as a result of complex interactions both within and external to the infant. What is of great importance during this time of rapid growth and change is how the infant's varied (and often intense) emotional states are recognised and nurtured by significant adults. These responses help create the neurobiological foundations for emotional development and the way the infant learns to manage their own emotions. (Conkbayir 2017)

Nurturing emotional literacy in the early years

To-day we hold the pupils in school, restricted by those instruments so degrading to body and spirit, the desk–and material prizes and punishments. Our aim in all this is to reduce them to the discipline of immobility and silence,–to lead them,–where? Far too often toward no definite end. **(Montessori 1912)**

The importance of balancing body and mind at an early age

The aim of this chapter is to begin to unpick the detail that we need in order to develop an understanding of 'emotional literacy', and what this requires of us in practice.

In order to do this we need to look at both the mind and the body as they are intrinsically linked in the way they affect emotions and how they are manifested.

The key words here are 'balancing body and mind'. This is because in order to understand a child emotionally it is vital that we understand how physically comfortable and confident they are alongside how they feel emotionally. We have to balance our thinking between reading emotional signs and physical signs.

How many situations are manifested emotionally, but are actually based in a physical cause? And vice versa. Understanding and supporting emotions means that we must inevitably be involved with working with **sensory** and **physical awareness**.

An example can be drawn from my personal experience as a child, when I was about six years old and I had to have several teeth removed as my mouth was overcrowded. This was a precursor to having a brace fitted. I do not have a fear of dentists, but to this day I do not like walking into car maintenance or bicycle

Chapter Two: Nurturing emotional literacy in the early years

shops, or anywhere that tyres are fitted, because of the smell of rubber. I had my teeth removed under general anaesthetic and a rubber mask was put over my face.

Songs, smells, tastes, and some things that we touch can bring back memories and emotions both good and bad. Reflect on the sensory things that affect you. How often do you have to deal with them? How do they affect you? Do you have coping strategies? If so, what are they? Do you know what things affect your colleagues, families, children in your care?

As you read, keep adding to the list of words that you started to create in Chapter One. Here we will examine how different emotions affect the whole body, making a physical, mental and sensory impact. With children starting settings and schools at very early ages this linking is important to understand. With this in mind this chapter falls into two sections: understanding the body and how this is inextricably linked to understanding the mind. In Chapter Three we will look at how 'emotional literacy' enables us to help children develop self-confidence and wellbeing.

Think about...

Is 'emotional literacy' the same as 'emotional intelligence'? As you work through each chapter record your thinking on this.

Case studies

Below are two case studies for comparison and discussion. As you read, reflect on how both physical and emotional aspects are manifested, and what would you do in both situations.

Case study: Geoffrey

Geoffrey found it very difficult to settle into his Reception Class. He was the youngest child of older parents. He had two grown up brothers. Geoffrey had never been to a setting before.

Physically, Geoffrey was smaller than his class mates. His speech was immature and he always spoke of himself in the third person. For example, 'Geoffrey wants to go to the toilet'. Everyday his Mum brought him to school and took him home again in a pushchair, holding his teddy bear which he brought into class with him.

Once he was in the school environment the other children either took no notice of him, or 'babied' him. He enjoyed the attention he received when he was in the role play area. The teaching staff found it difficult to engage him in learning opportunities because he struggled to focus or become engaged for any length of time. He found sitting or standing still hard, and was constantly moving, or lying on the floor.

Geoffrey was physically uncoordinated meaning that he did not enjoy or engage in physically active and challenging activity inside or out. He found getting dressed and undressed very hard, so when the whole class needed to get changed for PE sessions, he would take off all his clothes and stand naked until an adult helped him. This did not upset him, even when the other children laughed.

At snack and lunch times Geoffrey found feeding himself difficult. He wouldn't eat unless his food was mashed and fed to him from a spoon, and would only drink from a bottle or trainer cup. The lunch time staff were not happy about the situation and they often became annoyed. As a result Geoffrey could often be seen sitting by himself struggling with his lunch while all the other children sat together happily eating and socialising.

His Key Person had a conversation with Geoffrey's Mum about concerns and observations. Mum was not concerned and thought that, because he was much younger than his brothers, he was the 'baby of the family' and he acted accordingly. She felt that he would soon 'grow out of it'. The teacher accepted this, and Geoffrey remained the same.

Emotional Literacy in the early years

Chapter Two: Nurturing emotional literacy in the early years

> What do you notice here? What do you feel? There are several emotions shown in this story. What are they and who shows them? What would you do? How happy do you think Geoffrey actually was? What thinking from Chapter One can you apply here?

Use this next case study to reflect on your thinking and the conclusions you came to after reading about Geoffrey.

Case study: Scarlett

Scarlett was also the youngest child in her family, and she had grown up sisters. She was very quiet, always smiling and could often be found creating things in the workshop area. She had an eye for colour and liked to use lots of it in her work. She also had an eye for detail in her drawings. Although she was quiet, she was popular and was often to be seen engaged with the other children.

Part of the daily routine in this Reception Class was to take Teddy Edward home with his diary and overnight bag. The next morning everyone was excited to hear about his adventures. One day it was Scarlett's turn to take Teddy Edward home and she was delighted and ran out to her Mum clutching the overnight bag.

The next morning when the teacher welcomed all the children in, she noticed that Scarlett was in tears. Her friend Connor was comforting her. Connor explained to the teacher that, although she had taken the overnight bag home, Scarlett had actually forgotten Teddy Edward. The teacher felt really bad at this point as she had not noticed that the bear was still sitting on his special chair in the classroom.

Once all the children had gathered indoors the teacher told all the children what had happened and how both Scarlett and Teddy Edward were very upset. What could they all do to make it better? Connor leapt up and said they must have a party! Both adults in the room thought this was a great idea and the rest of the day was spent in preparation for the party that was held at the end of the afternoon. All the children made cakes, biscuits, hats, decorations, sandwiches, drinks, cards and invitations. Some went shopping with one of the teachers. Scarlett and Teddy Edward were the centre of attention, music played and everybody was engaged and enjoying themselves throughout the day and the party. The day ended with Scarlett delightedly making sure she had Teddy Edward with her this time.

> Compare Scarlett's story to that of Geoffrey. What are the similarities? What are the differences? What do you notice about how the children respond in each one? Also what do you notice about how the adults respond? What would you do?

Of all the people in the two case studies, which do you think demonstrated the most understanding of 'emotional literacy'? Why? How do you know?

Is 'emotional literacy' the same as 'emotional intelligence'?

If either of these two children joined your setting, what are the things that you would need to reflect on as a team in order not to judgmental?

After reading the case studies above, imagine that either of these two children joined your setting. What are the things that you would need to reflect on as a team in order not to be judgmental?

These two case studies illustrate how emotions affect the body and the mind. Those affected do not always make it obvious. Geoffrey appeared to show no emotion when the dinner ladies made him sit alone until he fed himself and finished eating. We can't know what he was actually feeling, but we know he should not have been treated differently.

Chapter Two: Nurturing emotional literacy in the early years

> **Remember...**
>
> We live in a world where there is an increasing recognition of emotional health and the impact it has on quality of life. We must view this recognition through two lenses;
>
> - Our core documents, both statutory and for guidance as they consistently remind us of this with references to personal, social and emotional development
> - Our own feelings and understandings as they will determine how we understand and interpret what we read.

Understanding the body – are you sitting comfortably?

It is no coincidence that physical development is high on the agenda of most, if not all, Early Years curricula. One of the three Prime Areas of the Statutory Framework for the Early Years Foundation Stage in England is personal, social and emotional development. (DfE 2017) states:

> Physical development involves providing opportunities for young children to be active and interactive; and to develop their co-ordination, control, and movement. Children must also be helped to understand the importance of physical activity (6), and to make healthy choices in relation to food.
>
> (6) The Chief Medical Office has published guidance on physical activity that providers may wish to refer to, which is available at: www.gov.uk/government/publications/uk-physical-activity-guidelines. (DfE 2017 p8)

However, despite being a core area of the EYFS (a Prime Area of Learning), the depth and extent of knowledge required to promote 'physical development' is not always understood. This is exemplified by the fact that the Chief Medical Officers guidelines are relegated to a footnote and clearly have not been used to inform the programme of study or the Early Learning Goal.

Understanding physical development means knowing more than the importance of gross motor skills, fine motor skills, healthy eating and exercise.

Whilst all of these are included in our various curricula they become distilled into little more than a simple tick list of skills, as, for example, can happen with those known as the 'Fundamental Motor Skills':

- Locomotor skills – such as running, jumping, hopping, galloping, skipping and leaping.
- Balance skills – movements where the body remains in place, but moves around its horizontal and vertical axes.
- Ball skills – such as catching, throwing, kicking, striking, underarm roll and striking.

Creating a list like this is of limited value as definitions using labels immediately narrows expectations and informed understanding.

Understanding how the body and mind, thus the emotions, are integral to each other, a wider definition of 'Physical Development' is required. This can be found on the website of the International Physical Literacy Association (IPLA) (www.physical-literacy.org.uk).

The definition given is:

> "Physical literacy can be described as the motivation, confidence, physical competence, knowledge and understanding to value and take responsibility for engagement in physical activities for life." (IPLA, 2017)

> Reflect on the words from the definition above:
>
> - **motivation**
> - **confidence**
> - **physical competence**
> - **understanding**.
>
> What do they mean to you?

We are beginning to make the link between mind and body and how they need to be balanced, otherwise negative feelings and emotions may be evoked.

Chapter Two: Nurturing emotional literacy in the early years

> ## Case study: A personal experience
>
> I am very short sighted and have been wearing glasses all the time since I was about six years old. When I reached senior school I was made to take my glasses off for every PE session whether it was outside, inside or swimming. As a result I couldn't see very well, so couldn't participate successfully and was never chosen for teams. The purpose of sharing this is because this experience has stayed with me – I still can't swim and I lack confidence in organised physical activity. I am sure that allowing me to wear my glasses would have meant that I would have had a very different attitude.
>
> It got to the point at school where I would hide in the library to avoid PE sessions altogether.
>
> Other than letting me wear my glasses, what would have been a more appropriate response from the teachers? What do you think they understood about their role?
>
> Thus I am not very physically confident, competent or motivated because of my experiences at school and the negative way that teachers responded to the situation. However, I am generally physically capable and can make my way in the world.
>
> What my teachers were lacking was an understanding of the concept of 'physical literacy' and that it is not just about physical fitness and development, or playing sport. It's also about understanding yourself and how you fit and interact with the world. Emotionally and Physically.
>
> This was summed up for me by my Tai Chi Teacher as the need to understand:
>
> - Physical Space – external physical space and how it feels
> - Inner space – how you handle your personal space – knowing your body and its feelings
> - Confident children are happy with, and in, their space as they understand their bodies inside and out
> - Staff and children must have the same understandings and notice when these are misaligned.
>
> The subtitle of this section is 'Are you sitting comfortably?'. Sitting still can be the hardest task we ask children to do. This can be frustrating for the child and the adults.

Have you ever stopped to think how many times a day you ask a child, or group, to 'sit still'? Start to make a note of how often you say this, and in what context.

What were you feeling? What might the children have been feeling? Could you have done anything differently?

At this point we need to become familiar with these two words and their definitions:

Proprioception - A baby's first playground is the floor. Lying on its back and kicking its legs, it learns to feel, as a result of movement, how long it is. By waving and spreading its arms, it starts to know how wide it is – this is called proprioceptive learning, or knowledge of the inner self, which is gained directly as a result of movement experience. (Goddard-Blythe, 2005)

Vestibular – Secure balance is inseparable from the development of postural control, which in turn is supported by information from the visual, proprioceptive, and motor systems.

Training of these systems is a gradual process during which maturation of the vestibular pathways involved will take until at least 7 years of age, and continue through puberty and beyond. Immature vestibular functioning is frequently found amongst children who have specific learning difficulties such as Dyslexia and Dyspraxia, problems of attention, language impairment, emotional problems, and adults who suffer from anxiety, Agoraphobia and Panic Disorder. (Goddard-Blythe, 2005)

Before we move into Chapter Three take time to reflect on the importance of balancing body and mind. The body is the host of all emotions, so it is essential that teachers are informed about physical development and what physical literacy means.

Chapter Two: Nurturing emotional literacy in the early years

Make sure that you understand the two definitions given above, and consider how they apply to your knowledge of the children you work with.

> …movement is an integral part of life from the moment of conception until death, and a child's experience of movement will play a pivotal part in shaping his personality, his feelings, and his achievements. Learning is not just about reading, writing, and maths. These are higher abilities that are built upon the integrity of the relationship between brain and body. (Goddard-Blythe, 2005)

This is a physically literate understanding of how the body and mind are linked. Conkbayir moves this idea forward by linking it to 'sensitive periods' of brain development. We'll examine this concept further in the next chapter.

> Take motor skills – babies and young children learn through the movement and coordination of their bodies. This movement not only strengthens muscles but also boosts brain development; controlling body movements leads to control of finer movements such as being able to manipulate and explore play materials and, later, learning how to write. It is difficult to master such fine motor skills if control over larger movements of the body is poor. If all young children are to successfully learn during sensitive periods, it makes sense that the concept of sensitive periods should be reflected across the early childhood curriculum provided in the setting. (Conkbayir 2017)

Before you start to read Chapter Three use your thinking from this chapter to reflect on the scenario below. As you read, remember the two 'lenses' introduced in Chapter One, filter your thinking through them:

- Our core documents, both statutory and for guidance as they consistently remind us of this with references to personal, social and emotional development
- Our own feelings and understandings as they will determine how we understand and interpret what we read.

Case study: On the playground

Every day the same core group of children, boys and girls, spent their time outside playing at being super heroes. This involved a great deal of rushing about, rugby tackling 'baddies' to the ground, and then wrestling with them until they 'surrendered'.

Other children joined in from time to time, but the for the most part the group remained the same. There were sometimes injuries and tears, but these incidents did not detract from the play, and the injured parties always joined back in.

There were two adults outside with the children. One was joining in some play, the other was watching the superhero play. Suddenly she blew a whistle and halted all the play, the other adult looked around surprised. It was announced that there was to be no more play fighting in the future.

What do you think is going on here? Physically and emotionally? What is your emotional response to this scenario? What happens at your setting?

Sensory cortex — Sensations
Parietal lobe — Perception, making sense of the world
Frontal lobe — Executive functions, thinking, planning, organising and problem solving, emotions and behavioural control, personality
Temporal lobe — Memory, understanding, language

When we reflect on the limbic system, the inextricable link between the brain and emotions becomes all the more clearer – our very being is governed by our emotional states (Conkbayir, 2017)

How emotional literacy supports wellbeing

We know only too well the sorry spectacle of the teacher who, in the ordinary schoolroom, must pour certain cut and dried facts into the heads of the scholars. In order to succeed in this barren task, she finds it necessary to discipline her pupils into immobility and to force their attention. Prizes and punishments are every-ready and efficient aids to the master who must force into a given attitude of mind and body those who are condemned to be his listeners. (Montessori 1912)

Helping children to develop self-confidence

In Chapter Two we started to reflect on the importance of balancing body and mind by beginning to examine how feeling comfortable – or uncomfortable – physically has an impact on our emotions. And how we, as emotionally literate teachers must understand this.

In this chapter we will move this thinking forward to consider wellbeing and self-confidence. This will involve looking in more detail at what we need to understand about how the brain works.

As you work through this chapter, remember to filter your thinking through:

- Our core documents, both statutory and for guidance, as they consistently remind us of this with references to personal, social and emotional development
- Our own feelings and understandings as they will determine how we understand and interpret what we read.

Chapter Three: How emotional literacy supports wellbeing

From this chapter onwards your reflection on the statements above will involve looking back through the previous chapters. Keep in mind that the physical and emotional are inextricably linked. We need to be alert to whether an emotion is related to a physical lack of confidence, or whether an emotion is being manifested physically.

> **Note**
>
> Keep adding to your list of words and expressions about feelings and emotions.

Sensitive periods

Working with children from birth to seven we are privileged to be part of nurturing them as their developing brains are at their most sensitive.

As teachers working with children during this crucial time for brain development, there are key things that we must be aware of to be sure that our practice is informed and appropriate. Above all, it is important to understand the principle that every child is individual, coming from their own families and cultures.

Being individual means that children go through stages of development in their own time, and what happens during these stages might impact on what happens next. Being aware of the sensitive periods of brain development and their optimum times, means that we can provide the best possible environments to support the children and their families.

Conkbayir explains:

> The concept of sensitive periods refers to distinct phases during early childhood when the brain is best able to receive and use information gained from experience, in order to learn specific skills. The period of birth to five specifically represents a sensitive period for babies and children as it represents a time of fervent growth and development, with neural connectivity being at its most prolific (Chugani 1998, as quoted in Conkbayir, 2017)

Conkbayir goes on to explain in depth the links between physical confidence and emotional wellbeing and confidence. This is because development of movement and coordination skills strengthens muscles and also boosts brain development.

Being comfortable with our bodies physically is a contributory factor to feeling emotionally secure. Chapter Two ended with a comment from Conkbayir on the importance of the limbic system, which she also calls 'the emotional brain'. It's the 'part of the brain concerned with the registering and storing of emotional information. This includes fear, anger and happiness' (Conkbayir 2017)

The link between physicality and emotions is farther shown here. Gerhardt (2015) notes that 'emotions are first and foremost our guides to action: they are about going towards things or going away from them'. This is important. Take some time to consider how you respond to things that engender emotions for you. In positive or negative ways. How do your emotions guide your actions?

> Children's emotional wellbeing is central to their overall well-being and identity. It is part of the brain's make-up, with its development being shaped

Chapter Three: How emotional literacy supports wellbeing

in response to the environment and the child's experience – be these positive or negative. Sroufe (1997 p25) explains:

> Maturation of the brain, including pathways for emotion and emotional regulation, is experience dependent, that is, social interactions directly influence central nervous development. (Conkbayir, 2017)

Using your reading from Chapter Two, reflect on what you have just read. Remember that Aga is four years old. Make notes on the actions of:

- The Teacher
- The Teaching Assistant
- The Visitor.

Look particularly at how emotions are demonstrated physically by each of them.

Reddy (2008) examines how young children perceive others 'in engagement'. She points out:

> Our perceptual experience of another person's frown or smile or tears, therefore, must always include in it our proprioceptive experience of our own bodily state

Case study: Aga

It was three weeks into the Summer Term and Aga, who had just moved from Poland, was new to the Reception class in a one form entry school in a small village. She was four years old and did not speak English.

The children had all been sitting on the carpet listening to the teacher since they had arrived at school. This was now forty minutes ago. As the visitor watched the children were told that they could leave the carpet and 'choose' what they wanted to do.

Aga wandered for a while then found her way over to where the visitor was in the role play 'café'. A group of children had approached the visitor to 'open' the café as it was new to them and the class teacher had not mentioned it. The visitor was now engaged with a group ordering food and drink and writing menus.

Aga sidled up, and snuggled into the visitor who noticed that she was quietly sobbing. As Aga had very little English, and was visibly upset, it was difficult to establish what was wrong. However she kept repeating the word 'phonics'. Keeping the little girl with her, the visitor went over to the teacher who was hearing a child read, to see if she could shed any light on the problem. She was informed that in a few minutes the children would be called back to the carpet for the daily phonics session. On hearing this Aga became visibly more upset. She had worked out the regular pattern of the morning and knew that 'choosing time' probably meant that phonics would come next. A bell signalled the time for all the children to gather. Aga would not let go of the visitor, who then sat on the carpet with her.

The children were all grouped together for the phonics teaching. The session began. Aga snuggled up to the visitor, she was trembling and sobbing quietly. The visitor pointed this out to a Teaching Assistant who was sitting nearby, who responded that this happened every day and that Aga would get over it. The Teaching Assistant indicated a chair and suggested that the visitor moved away to sit on it. The offer was politely declined.

To begin with Aga relaxed a little. The teacher was revising Phase Two sounds and she knew some of them, but the Teacher was not looking in her direction. As the session went on, and the Teacher moved onto Phases Three and Four, Aga's agitation resulted in her needing the toilet urgently. Her stomach was rumbling, and she was suddenly very uncomfortable. This added to her distress. She left the room. By the time she got back the phonics session was over.

Aga remained unsettled for the rest of the morning and she kept close to the visitor.

Chapter Three: How emotional literacy supports wellbeing

and, most importantly, our affective and motivational state. Conversely, our proprioceptive experience of our own acts and reactions and feelings always involves the perception of what relevant others are doing, saying or feeling. (Reddy 2008)

A core part of our role is that we help the children to build wellbeing and self-confidence. Understanding perception and proprioception, as it applies to ourselves and those we work with is key.

Wellbeing

As the responsible adults in the environment we must be sure that we model and project a feeling of wellbeing.

Ferre Laevers has described the child with a high level of wellbeing as one who feels 'like a fish in water'. In other words the child is comfortable in their own skin, and more often than not confident in how they are with others. Physically and emotionally, their bodies and minds are balanced.

> As per Laevers' definition, do you think that Aga felt 'like a fish in water'? Write down your reasons and add to your list of words that describe feelings and emotions.

Professor Laevers and his team have developed the Leuven Scales of Wellbeing and Involvement. In the next Chapter we'll unpick these further as we look at the role of the adult in fostering emotional literacy.

Not waving, but drowning

If we are going to understand wellbeing and self-confidence in the children and families we work with, as well as our colleagues, we need to be informed about what may have an impact. This may be either positively or negatively.

> Observe the children in your setting. Do you know if they are feeling confident? Happy? How do you know? What is the evidence?

It is all too easy in a busy setting with all the pressures we feel daily to forget that we are all human, and that not everything is the same all the time.

> **Remember...**
>
> Reflect on the things that may have a negative impact on wellbeing and self-confidence. Would the same things affect the adults as the children? Remember that things could be happening within a family that they may not have shared with the child, or us, but the child will pick up on moods. This will be the same for difficult situations within the setting.

It is very easy to fall into the trap of labelling a child based on how they present themselves to us. Is the self confident child really that confident? How do we know whether the child who seems to feel comfortable actually has a sense of wellbeing?

Go back to the Case Study about Connor and Scarlett in Chapter Two. As you read it again reflect on how confident you think each child was and how you know.

Chapter Three: How emotional literacy supports wellbeing

Do you think that each child had a sense of wellbeing. How do you know? What effect did they have on each other?

How did the teacher interpret the situation? Compare how she responded to how the adults reacted in the Case Study about Aga, in this chapter.

Case study

As you read, reflect on the self-confidence and wellbeing of both Aaron and Charlie in the next case study. Consider how they demonstrated these, and what the adults did to support.

Case study: Aaron and Charlie

It was the end of the Summer Term and the children who would be starting in the Reception classes the following September were visiting the school with their families to have their 'taster sessions'. The children went to their new classes to mix with some of the current children and the adults that they would be working with. Tea and coffee was available in the Hall for the families who were free to sit and wait, or pop in to see how it was going in the Reception environments. The Team had not set up any specific activities and the normal 'free flow' session was running. This meant that all the teachers could observe, play and interact with all the children and get to know their new cohort. This was the third, and final, visit – they had taken place over three weeks on different days so maximise the opportunities for as many families as possible to attend at least one.

Aaron had been to all three sessions with his Mum, but this was Charlie's first visit. Charlie was the oldest of three children and Aaron an only child. They had not met before, and neither had been to a Nursery or Preschool setting. By coincidence, they both had March birthdays so they were still four years old. Both entered the room happily and their Mums went to have a cup of tea. As Aaron had been before he knew that he wanted to go to the outdoor area. Charlie started exploring. First observations would suggest that they both appeared self confident and with no issues with wellbeing. However first impressions were misleading.

During his first visit the team noticed that, although happy to chat and play with the other children, Aaron stopped talking if he noticed an adult nearby. This was observed through all of his visits. The teachers tried a couple of approaches, such as playing alongside and chatting with the group, and even noticing that he always wore his favourite shirt for the visits. One of the teachers had a similar one that she wore when she knew he was coming. But nothing encouraged him to speak to anyone other than the children or his Mum.

On the other hand, Charlie came straight in and happily engaged with adults and children alike. He was interested in football and knew a lot about West Ham Football Club. He loved to talk about his interest to anyone who would listen. This was later to mean that his teachers had to brush up on their knowledge. Aaron and Charlie teamed up almost immediately with Aaron showing Charlie around and helping him out with finding things. This friendship was still in place when the all the children started school full time the following September. However Aaron would still only speak to those of his own age. It soon became clear that Aaron and Charlie made a good team. Aaron would tell Charlie want he wanted to say and he would be his voice in conversation with adults. The teachers learnt a lot this way and were happy to let this continue. Working in partnership with Aaron's Mum, they had no concerns about his all round development. No pressure was put on Aaron.

Towards the end of the Spring Term, when both boys had recently had their fifth birthdays, all the children were returning to the classroom from their lunch break. There was lots of chatter. Charlie and Aaron came in together, Aaron slightly ahead. As he walked in he turned, smiled at the teacher and said 'Good afternoon Mrs A.' He had a big smile on his face. Charlie rushed up and said 'Aaron! You spoke!' He was delighted for his friend. After that Aaron was happy to interact with everyone.

Chapter Three: How emotional literacy supports wellbeing

Having read this case study, what are your thoughts about Charlie and Aaron and how they reacted to situations? What would you say about the way the adults responded to both children? What did you fell about Aaron not speaking to adults?

You may have added more words to your list of vocabulary. If you have, were these words positive or negative?

This chapter has been concerned with understanding how 'emotional literacy' supports wellbeing and develops children's self-confidence. Reflecting on Aaron's situation is an interesting one here. It would have been very easy to jump to the conclusion that he had a 'special need'. In fact there was never any clear reason for why he didn't speak. It could have been lack of confidence or security, but the teachers, working with Mum, could never reach a conclusion.

As he moved through Primary School each new teacher was informed that he may not speak, but this trait had disappeared by the time he reached Year Three.

Part of being emotionally literate means that we must not be quick to judge or make assumptions. Understanding what is meant by a confident child whose wellbeing is secure means not jumping to conclusions. Thus we must avoid:

- Making judgements on very young children
- Seeing 'poor behaviour' rather than investigating what may be really happening
- Labelling children as a 'special need' as soon as we meet them
- Judging families and parenting styles.

Think about...

Is 'emotional literacy' the same as 'emotional intelligence'? How has reading this chapter added to your thinking?

As you reflect on this chapter, consider the children you work with and how they express their feelings and emotions. How do you enable this to happen? Does everyone on the team respond the same way?

Emotional Literacy in the early years

The role of the adult

The environment you construct around you and the children also reflects this image you have about the child. There's a difference between the environment that you are able to build based on a preconceived image of the child and the environment that you can build that is based on the child you see in front of you — the relationship you build with the child, the games you play. An environment that grows out of your relationship with the child is unique and fluid. The quality and quantity of relationships among you as adults and educators also reflects your image of the child. **(Malaguzzi www.reggioalliance.org)**

Fostering emotional literacy in the setting

How often have you walked into your setting with a smile on your face, but inside you are very emotional about something that has happened in your personal life that you won't allow to affect you professionally? The emotion could be caused by anything, maybe positive or negative, or you may not even know why you are feeling like you do, you just know that you can't allow your feelings to show.

> Reflect on the quote from Malaguzzi that opens this chapter. How can you apply it to your setting and environment?
>
> In the Appendix at the end of the book, there is an audit tool based on this that can be used to inform a team meeting to help develop thinking.

Malaguzzi goes on to write:

And it is the same for you as adults. When you enter the school in the morning, you carry with you pieces of your life — your happiness, your sadness, your hopes, your pleasures, the stresses from your life. You never come in an isolated way; you always

Chapter Four: The role of the adult

come with pieces of the world attached to you. So the meetings that we have are always contaminated with the experiences that we bring with us.

The use of the word 'contaminated' in the quote suggests that every emotion that impacts on our work is negative, it won't always be.

I'm sure that we have all been through times when our emotions were running high and we needed friends and colleagues to be able to read the situation. I know I have. My class environment and my immediate colleagues were my security blanket when it was often difficult to cross the threshold. I could lose myself in the work I enjoyed and not worrying for a few hours. This was not easy, but as an adult I had learnt the idea of 'leaving my baggage at the door'. My closest colleagues understood.

The children we work with come from all sorts of backgrounds and situations, even those we assume to be the most settled can go through unsettling times for all sorts of reasons. Someone once said to me that if your eyes don't light up when you see the children then you're in the wrong job. The children must be able to see and feel that about us so that we can be their security blankets.

This is not to suggest that this is easy for any of us.

Reflect on all the case studies that you have read so far. Look again at the way the adults behaved. Do you think that they always felt their eyes light up when they saw their children every day? Do you? What would help in this situation?

The role of all the adults is to foster an emotionally secure environment where adults and children alike feel like, to use Professor Laevers' term, 'fish in water'. So there are two viewpoints to an emotionally secure environment – that of the adult, then that of the children.

Remember to filter your thinking through:

- Our core documents, both statutory and for guidance as they consistently remind us of this with references to personal, social and emotional development
- Our own feelings and understandings as they will determine how we understand and interpret what we read.

> Keep adding to your list of words and expressions about feelings and emotions.

How do you see yourself?

I often ask early years practitioners what they understand to be their role in working with young children. This has led to many interesting points and been the basis of much discussion.

Make a comprehensive list of what you feel your role to be. What is at the top of your list? Is your list hierarchical? Do you think it should be? Remember that, whatever our qualification, we are all teachers.

> **Think about...**
>
> Now that you have unpicked your role, how do you feel about what you have written. Are you happy with it all? Are there things you would like to change to enable you to feel better?

Emotional Literacy in the early years

Chapter Four: The role of the adult

Whenever Professor Laevers writes using the word 'children' it is useful to substitute the word 'adult' so that we can reflect on ourselves and those around us.

> When we want to know how each of the children is doing in a setting, we first have to explore the degree in which children do feel at ease, act spontaneously, show vitality and self-confidence. All this indicates that their emotional well-being is ok and that their physical needs, the need for tenderness and affection, the need for safety and clarity, the need for social recognition, the need to feel competent and the need for meaning in life and moral value are satisfied.

> The second criterion – involvement - is linked to the developmental process and urges the adult to set up a challenging environment favouring concentrated, intrinsically motivated activity. Care settings and schools have to succeed on both tasks: only paying attention to emotional well-being and a positive climate is not enough, while efforts to enhance involvement will only have an impact if children and students feel at home and are free from emotional constraints.

Center for Experiential Education – February 2015

The Leuven Scales of Wellbeing and Involvement are key tools here. All too often these scales are seen as a 'tick box' exercise that is completed as an 'assessment'. Some electronic trackers include them, and copies of 'assessment sheets' are freely available to download. However, it is really important that appropriate training is in place before using the Leuven Scales to develop your understanding of practice. This is not the place to go into detail about the scales other than to recommend that you find out more as the training will further underpin your development of a consistent approach to maintaining 'emotional literacy'. An important starting point in this understanding is the following:

> Children with a high level of well-being feel great. They enjoy life to the full. They have fun, take joy in each other and in their surroundings. They radiate vitality as well as relaxation and inner peace. They adopt an open and receptive attitude towards their environment. They are spontaneous and can fully be themselves. Well-being is linked to self-confidence, a good degree of self-esteem and resilience. All this is based on being in touch with themselves, with their own feelings and experiences, fresh and pure. (Laevers 2005)

Chapter Four: The role of the adult

> What affects your self-esteem?
>
> As you read, keep in mind that wellbeing means feeling 'like a fish in water', and that we are part of enabling this feeling.

> How would you describe what happened here? What would you have done? If you had been the visitor how would you have approached the situation with the team to discuss this?

Case study: Settling in - the first day at the nursery

It was the first time that the little boy had been left at the setting – he had previously visited with his Mum, but she had left him there this time. The family did not speak English and had not been in the area very long. He was three years old.

He would not take his coat off and it was buttoned right up to his neck. It was about 10.30am meaning that he had been at the preschool for an hour and a half. All that time he had been wandering around quietly whimpering and talking to himself. A visitor had just arrived to do some observations and this had upset him as he had thought it was his Mum coming back. The visitor enquired as to which member of the team was his Key Person. An adult was indicated. She was sitting at a table with her back to the child working with a group.

As the visitor watched, the little boy continued to wander as his Key Person finished with her group and started to set the table up for snack time. No one was interacting with the little boy.

Children were called over for snack and the Key Person sat with them. All the chairs around the table were filled.

Suddenly the little boy noticed where his Key Person was. He stopped whimpering, found a spare chair and dragged over to be next to her. She turned, saw him and told him he couldn't put his chair there as there was no room, although a space could easily have been made. He pulled the chair back to where he had found it and started whimpering again.

Consistency in emotional literacy

The role of the Key Person is pivotal in demonstrating and promoting emotional literacy for the children. Consistency is not easy to maintain however. This is evident every day in public adult displays of behaviour.

Case study: Managing feelings

Just recently I witnessed a row in a coffee shop that seemingly came from nowhere. Four men were not happy about something they had bought so they confronted the staff behind the counter. The staff acted calmly and asked not to be spoken to like that but to no avail.

The young Manager came out and asked the men to leave but they returned to their seats and she followed them repeating her request. In the end she gave up and went back to her office. The men sat and talked amongst themselves for a while, complaining about their treatment, then went to the coffee shop up the road.

> There is a lot going on here. In light of what of the chapters you've read so far, what are your thoughts? If the group of men had been a group of children what might have happened?

As teachers in Early Years settings we work with similar situations on daily basis. The role of the Key Person for the child is to:

> ...accept their emotions and respond with understanding.

Chapter Four: The role of the adult

Grenier et al go on to note:

> This does not mean condoning negative or anti-social behaviours but by acknowledging the feelings that may underlie such behaviours such as anger, anxiety, distress or jealousy gives children the message that we empathise with their difficulties even when we do not approve of their method of expressing them. Providing vocabulary for feelings will support children to become aware of their emotions.

All children, indeed all adults, deserve respect. Reflect this against the behaviour of the adults in the coffee shop. Fisher (2016) goes further to define the role as:

> …knowing about the child's prior experiences and knowledge gives practitioners vital information for responding to and scaffolding their attempts to learn while planning appropriately and meaningfully for the next stages of their learning.

To build these relationships requires trust, flexibility, time, sharing and acknowledging that others have valid opinions too. Including the children. Consistency in a emotionally literate approach also requires that we have confidence in our pedagogy. We will return to our pedagogical approach in Chapters Seven and Eight.

Working together in a truly collaborative way

Unfortunately it is still the case that teachers can be seen as very judgemental. Whilst none of us like to admit to this, if we are honest then we have probably all been guilty of viewing children through the 'halo and horns' effect, or made too easy and quick judgement about a child based on thier appearance or family.

> The 'halo and horns' effect trap is easy to fall into. How often have you judged a child, or family, on their appearance at first meeting? What prompted your judgement? How did it affect your future relationship with the child or family?

This is human nature and, no matter what we do, with the best will in the world at some point we are all going to find ourselves in situations where we can't get along with particular people. Just as well there will be occasions when we are having to relate with people who simply don't like us. We are also subject to so many pressures that affect our self-esteem and professional status. For example:

- If we work term time only we can be perceived as part-time
- Working with the youngest children can mean we are seen as 'babysitters'
- As teachers in Early Childhood Education there is a perception that our role is not as important as that of teachers in Primary and Secondary education.

> What have you noticed having an impact on your emotional wellbeing as a professional? Have you managed to stop this impact affecting your work? If so, what helped? These focuses may help your thinking:
>
> - Expectations
> - Personal feelings
> - Assumptions
> - Outside influences
> - Other people.

Chapter Four: The role of the adult

Fisher (2016) writes of the importance of 'an emotional space for the practitioner':

> In order for practitioners to create a safe, emotional space in which children and their parents can thrive, they also need to ensure that their working environment is emotionally supportive of them as individuals. (Fisher, J. 2016)

The role of the Key Person can be emotionally challenging, as can every aspect of working in a team of any size. Fisher points out that it should be the right of every teacher to have regular private discussion time with a 'mentor, manager or senior teacher' to talk and 'offload'. We all need to know that some 'has got our back' when we are struggling.

The requirement to have regular meetings, or 'supervisions' as they are sometimes called, is important.

3.22. Supervision should provide opportunities for staff to:

- discuss any issues – particularly concerning children's development or wellbeing, including child protection concerns
- identify solutions to address issues as they arise
- receive coaching to improve their personal effectiveness.
(DfE 2017)

> Use the second of the two lenses of reflection to review your experience of 'supervisions':
>
> 'Our own feelings and understandings as they will determine how we understand and interpret what we read'
>
> Consider how 'supervisions' work in your setting. How do you feel before the meeting? And after?
>
> If you are a in a leadership role, how do you manage each meeting? Is yours managed in similar way?

Before moving onto thinking how emotional literacy impacts our work with parents, consider these statements:

When practitioners feel good about themselves they are in the best place to support others, in turn, to feel good. I like O'Connor's (2014) analogy with the oxygen masks in an aeroplane: adults who do not put on their own mask first are not in a position to help those more vulnerable people who are relying on them. (Fisher 2016)

Once we begin to look at the way adults interact with children we realise how powerful these dimensions are. In view of getting high levels of well-being and involvement the adult is even more important than other dimensions of the context, such as the space, the material and the activities on offer. Center for Experiential Education – February 2015

> **Time to reflect:**
> Think about the case studies on settling in on the first day at the nursery and managing feelings and ask yourself: Is 'emotional literacy' the same as 'emotional intelligence'?

Emotional Literacy in the early years

Working in partnership with parents

We must forge strong alliances with the families of our children. Imagine the school as an enormous hot air balloon. The hot air balloon is on the ground when the parents bring their children in the morning. Some parents think the balloon is going to rise up and fly around during the day. Others would really prefer that the balloon remain on the ground because that way they are sure their children are safe and protected. But the children want to go up and fly and travel everywhere in a hot air balloon, to see in this different way, to look at things from above. **(Malaguzzi www.reggioalliance.org)**

Understanding what went before

This chapter is inextricably linked to the previous one as it centres on adult relationships. However, in this instance the adults are entrusting us to look after their child. Malaguzzi's balloon analogy is a very powerful one about varying expectations. But it paints a simplistic view of families and their children, with an assumption that the only difference we encounter every day is whether the children 'rise up and fly' or 'remain on the ground'. Our reality is more complicated.

Our statutory documents require us to work in partnership with parents.

That the Early Years Foundation Stage made 'partnership working between practitioners and with parents and/or carers' a statutory requirement has been troublesome as it is not as straightforward as it sounds. Families have many more ideas of what the balloon should, and should not, be and where it should go than the opening would suggest:

Parents' aspirations for their children tell us a lot about their personal and cultural beliefs and values,

Chapter Five: Working in partnership with parents

and about reasons why they bring their children up as they do. Children may not always turn out the way their parents wish them to, but parents' conceptions of their children's future underpin every aspect of family life and values: basically, families behave in ways calculated (consciously or unconsciously) to bring about the ends they desire, and rear their children in the light of their own views on what a good outcome for the child might be.
(Brooker L. 2002)

Remember to filter your thinking through:

- Our core documents, both statutory and for guidance as they consistently remind us of this with references to personal, social and emotional development
- Our own feelings and understandings as they will determine how we understand and interpret what we read.

I remember once at a parents' evening Ryan's Dad telling me proudly that his son knew all the multiplication tables up to the twelve times table. This was the first parents evening of the year for my Reception Class. I was talking to Ryan's parents about what my on entry observations had taught me about their son, and how he was settling into school. I had seen no evidence of Ryan being as secure with numbers as his Dad thought.

> Read the opening quote again and reflect on the families that you engage with on a daily basis. Jot down how you work with parents to help them to 'understand the importance of what the teachers and children are doing in the hot air balloon'. What are the obstacles and how do you overcome them?

Reflecting on everything you have read in previous chapters, how would you have responded to this?

'We must forge strong alliances'

This is a powerful statement, and forging these alliances requires that, as a team, we have consistency of understanding of emotional literacy. This is particularly important as there are several strands of this work that may involve displays of emotion. Sobel (2019) writes:

> …working with parents generates a host of challenging factors, especially the need for 'balance' between schools and parents. Research tells us that for teachers and school leadership teams, dealing with two opposing groups of parents, those on the outside and those who are over-involved, is a cause of considerable stress.
> (Sobel 2019)

He then goes on to point out:

> Home stability is the cornerstone of a child's wellbeing. School is the vital partner. Schools need to work alongside parents offering them transparency in their approach and varied opportunities to become involved.
> (Sobel 2019)

Whilst we cannot guarantee home stability, we must make every effort to provide daily stability in our settings. For the families and the children. How do we do this?

We need to remember that it is impossible to get on with everyone, but as emotionally literate adults and professionals this does not affect our role.

Revise the thinking you did for Chapter Four, and how substituting the word 'adult' for the word 'child' in what we read can be very powerful. If you were the Key Person for Ryan's Dad in the example above how would you respond?

Would you see him as having a 'halo' or 'horns'? How would you justify your opinion?

Make a list of all the current vocabulary that is used daily to describe children and families. For example 'hard to reach' or 'below age related expectations'. How does using this vocabulary affect how you see the children?

Part of the expectations of working in partnership with parents is that we support them with understanding the importance of the 'home learning environment (HLE)'. For this to be effective we all have to understand what is important in the 'hot air balloon' of our setting.

Chapter Five: Working in partnership with parents

> Make a list of what you feel is important in your setting, and what you feel the parents need to know.
>
> What do you understand as 'home learning' and how does this fit in with what happens in your setting? How does it fit with what you know of the home lives of the children?
>
> Has focusing on emotional literacy changed your thinking?

Keep adding to your list of words and expressions about feelings and emotions.

Many young children live lives that are far removed from the experiences of those who work with them. It is so important that every practitioner comes to understand each of their children as individuals who have their own personal histories and their own unique personalities that are formed, influentially, by their parents and the circumstances into which they are born. If judgements are made about children and their families, based on the yardstick of practitioners' own lives, then any child who falls outside of those narrow parameters may sense feelings of alienation or disapproval from the very practitioner with whom they are meant to forge a close relationship. (Fisher, J. 2016)

Notice that the word 'learning' is not used here, but what is described is actually all about things that are learnt. All the things that are learnt through feelings and emotions. Why do some children thrive at school when others struggle to succeed?

Compare the quote from Fisher with this from Brooker (2002):

> All of children's early experience – from being picked up and cuddled, fed and changed, rocked and soothed, to being taken to the library or shown how to count – is a form of learning, and all the All Saints' children had acquired an incalculable amount of knowledge before starting school. (Brooker, 2002)

Both authors are reflecting on the importance of the 'home learning experience' and how we must be sensitive to the previous experiences of the child.

Cultural capital

The expression 'cultural capital' has recently become much more commonly used, as such it is one that we must be secure in understanding.

Put simply 'cultural capital' means all the experiences that have made us who we are. So our background, traditions and beliefs that shape our perceptions of life and how we live it. The theory was originally constructed by the French Social Theorist Bordieu:

> He sees this cultural capital as a 'habitus', a social tendency or disposition to act, think, or feel in a particular way. By analogy with economic capital, such resources can be invested and accumulated and can be converted into other forms. Thus, middle class parents are able to endow their children with the linguistic and cultural competences that will give them a greater likelihood of success at school and at university. Working-class children, without access to such cultural resources, are less likely to be successful in the educational system. http://www.oxfordreference.com

Chapter Five: Working in partnership with parents

Robin Alexander (2004) explains 'culture' as:

- culture: the web of values, ideas, institutions and processes which inform, shape and explain a society's views of education, teaching and learning, and which throw up a complex burden of choices and dilemmas for those whose job it is to translate these into a practical pedagogy;
- self: what it is to be a person, an individual relating to others and to the wider society, and how through education and other early experiences selfhood is acquired.

It is vital that we value the 'cultural capital' that everyone brings to the setting, and that we include it in the mix that informs our 'emotional literacy'. As Alexander notes, this is complex. But it is pivotal to understanding 'emotional literacy' that we are not judgmental. We must celebrate the diversity and uniqueness of all we meet and work with.

In order to form a mutually comfortable, emotionally literate, partnership with parents and families, what we need to understand is the 'cultural capital' that all children and families bring with them. And we need to understand our own alongside it.

The expression 'cultural capital' is increasingly familiar since it became part of Ofsted documentation. The types of 'cultural capital' we all bring with us can differ widely. Some of this capital will be perceived as 'ready for school' and 'acceptable', but not all of it necessarily will be.

> Middle-class children's early acquisition of cultural capital (Bourdieu believes) derives its effect from 'the amount of time devoted to acquiring it', which depends in part on the family's financial ability to contribute that time to the child's early education. Families from lower social groups, though not providing the same cultural environment as the dominant classes, can nevertheless prioritise the effort to give their child 'a gain in time, a head start' by transmitting what knowledge they have to the child in the years before school. Cultural capital requires above all a lengthy period of acquisition, and it is too late to catch up when the child begins statutory schooling. (Brooker 2002)

Case study

As you read think about what is meant by 'cultural capital' and how it applies to both these families. What sort of relationship do you think the families had with the teachers and the school? What would you do with the information the teachers found out?

Case study: Ricky

Ricky had never been away from his family before he started in the Reception Class. He had two older sisters who were already in school so he was familiar with the setting and had met the Reception Team. However he didn't know any of the other children.

He kept himself to himself and played with cars and trains. From their observations the teachers were coming to the conclusion that Ricky was not that familiar with books and numbers.

One day a teacher was playing alongside Ricky when he picked up a toy racing car and started talking about Formula One motor racing. He talked about the different makes of cars, knew the names of all the drivers, which team they drive for and where they came from in the world.

Case study: Jordan

Jordan lived with his Mum, Stepdad and little brother. Just like Ricky, he had never been to a nursery or preschool. When the teachers went for the home visit his Mum told them how excited Jordan was and he wanted them to go through to the garden. Whilst his Stepdad was working on an engine in the shed, Jordan was riding his own, real, motorbike round the garden. He was kitted out in leathers and a helmet.

Once he had shown the teachers his motorbike, he took them indoors to show them his Mum's pet rat. As with Ricky, Jordan showed no interest in literacy and numeracy when he started school.

Chapter Five: Working in partnership with parents

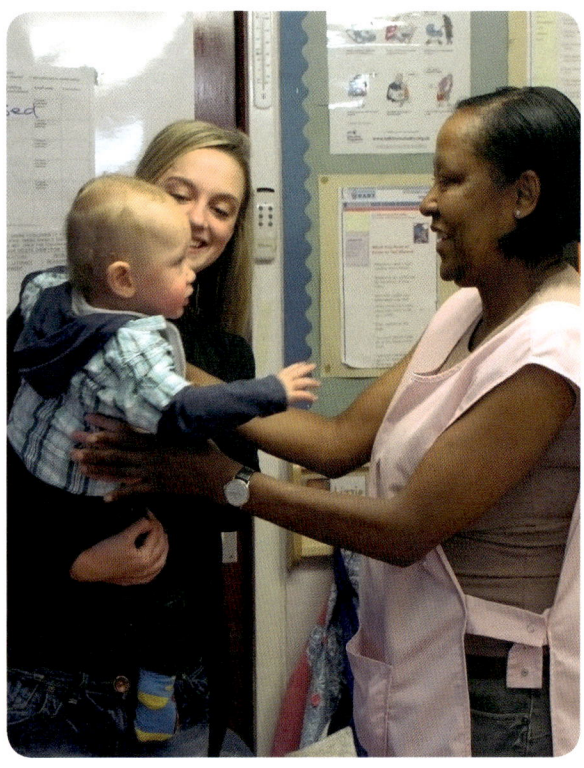

Case study: Lana's Mum

Lana lived with her Mum and little brother in a tiny bedsit over a shop. The family had been through difficult times and had escaped an abusive relationship. Lana's Mum was very embarrassed by the situation that she found herself in, it was not how she had seen herself bringing up the children. When the time came for Lana to start school her Mum declined the home visit. She gave no reason at that point.

Despite being relatively new to the area Lana settled well in the Reception class. The observations the teachers made showed her to have a good understanding of numeracy and literacy which they were happy to report to her Mum at parent's evening. Mum was very relieved to hear this, and she shared her story. She had been worried that Lana would be struggling with everything that had happened. She apologised about not having a home visit. Once the teachers knew all of this one of them regularly met Lana's Mum. These meetings were held at a local coffee shop so that the baby could come too and it would be a more relaxed chat.

Self-fulfilling prophecies

Of course it would be wonderful if all children came to us from happy and stable backgrounds, but it is not for us to define what 'happy and stable' looks like, or to judge if a background isn't the same as our own. If we judge we find that what happens is likely to become a self-fulfilling prophecy.

Look back at the words and phrases you jotted down at the beginning of the chapter. The labels that are fashionably used to describe families and children are very unhelpful in helping us to really understand and form trusting relationships.

In conversations with teachers about forming effective partnerships we have coined the phrase 'situational compassion'. This means the ability to sense the positive in every situation and work with it. Making assumptions and attaching labels when we know nothing about a family will send them powerful messages that we did not intend to give.

Time to reflect:
Take time to reflect again on what you understand by 'emotional literacy' and ask yourself: is it the same as 'emotional intelligence'?

How emotional literacy supports an inclusive environment

Temper tantrums may be stirred up not only by unexpected interferences by the environment, such as not getting what he wants or being told to do something he does not wish to do, but by disappointments at his own failures and insufficiencies and exasperation at not being understood. (Isaacs 1937)

An emotionally literate provision

A separate chapter on supporting an 'inclusive environment' feels contradictory to the message of inclusion, however there is an important reason for putting the book together like this. This chapter acts as a punctuation point to pull together everything written so far before moving on to discussing how to create an appropriate and effective 'emotionally literate' environment.

So far, the clear messages have been of working to understand individual feelings and how best to support and enable them in positive ways. This work applies to the feelings of adults and children alike. This ethos immediately suggests how an 'inclusive environment' should feel. If we refer to each child as a 'unique child', and we say that we know that 'one size does not fit all', then we must demonstrate this in our practice.

Working with the youngest children puts us in the best position to provide and promote an emotionally literate and inclusive environment. Use your reflections from the previous five chapters to inform your thinking now. Should 'emotional literacy' mean something different in an 'inclusive environment'? Remember to filter your thinking through:

- Our core documents, both statutory and for guidance as they consistently remind us of this with references to personal, social and emotional development
- Our own feelings and understandings as they will determine how we understand and interpret what we read.

Chapter Six: How emotional literacy supports an inclusive environment

The inclusive environment

Creating developmentally appropriate emotional and physical provision is core to our roles in Early Childhood Education. This must also be an inclusive environment. Children all have differing needs, and these must be enabled. This section includes the work of a playgroup that is respected for its provision for children with particular needs.

> Reflecting on what you have read so far, do you think that an emotionally literate 'inclusive' environment would look like? Why?

Below is an observation made in a preschool that is well known for the strength of the work they do to include children with special needs and disabilities.

The preschool is situated in a purpose built unit in the grounds of a large primary school.

Ever since it opened the group has been gaining a good reputation for the work they do for all children, and particularly their support and inclusion of all children and families. A morning spent observing practice and talking to the children and staff resulted in these key points of practice. As you read, reflect on your thinking about 'emotional literacy' and how the team at this setting could be seen to be demonstrating it;

- The 'settling in' process is given time. The children are observed and the Key Person is only allocated once the team know who the child and family feel comfortable with
- The team speak about the qualities of building trust and 'forming a bond'.
- All interactions take place at the level of the child so that eye contact is made
- The team is all trained to use signing, and the children sign too
- The names of the children are used in all interactions
- The body language used by the team is open and receptive
- Everyone smiles
- The choices of the children are respected
- Visual timetables and clues are used at times of transition
- When choices are given they are clearly named and described according to the needs of the child
- No one is rushed
- The routines are clear, understood and relevant
- When a teacher is working with a small group on communication skills, each child is actively included and is enabled to make a choice. The contribution of each child is mirrored back to the others in the group. Turn taking was reinforced
- The individual needs of each child are known by all the team so that everyone can support targets
- All the teachers and children have a role in tidying up, and every child is expected to be as independent as possible
- The environment is uncluttered and resourcing is clear
- All children are treated equally
- Reasonable adjustments are made
- Connections are made with the families and all the schools the children transfer to.

> Use this list to audit your provision. Are there actions that you need to take? Why and how will you evidence them?

Early intervention

A child's Key Person is central to an inclusive environment. Notice how the playgroup chooses the Key Person for each child. This relationship must be right as they may be the first person to notice something about a child. There are all sorts of reasons for this – it may that the child has not been away from the care of the family before, the family are new to the country, or the child has not mixed with children of a similar age. The role of the Key Person has been discussed in Chapter Four. Review this Chapter before reading this case study.

Case study

> As you read this case study reflect on 'emotional literacy' and whether this is an 'inclusive environment'.

There is a lot to discuss in this case study in areas other than that of emotional literacy.

Chapter Six: How emotional literacy supports an inclusive environment

Case study: Michael

Michael arrived in the Reception Class and seemed to settle in straight away. He had never been to a preschool setting or toddler group, and was the oldest child in his family. He had a baby sister.

Michael was surrounded by a very caring extended family and was looked after by them when his parents were at work. No concerns were raised by the parents, and the teachers did not immediately pick up on anything.

As time went by however the team began to notice things through their observations. Michael was a tall, well built child. Not overweight, but obviously bigger than the others in his group. He could easily have been mistaken for older than his years.

It became increasingly obvious that Michael moved awkwardly in some situations. The extent of the potential problem was not picked up straight away, although the team were becoming aware that he was not very agile, or spatially aware. It was when the class went on a day trip to a venue where lots of stairs were involved that the concern of the teachers came to a head. The school did not have stairs, so the team had not been aware that Michael was only able to climb up and down on all fours, or by dragging himself up holding tightly to the banister.

As soon as they had returned from the day out observations were written and decisions made. The team had worked with a child with dyspraxia before so they decided that this was probably the same thing.

The School Welfare Assistant and the School Nurse were asked to observe and give their opinions. All agreed that dyspraxia was probably the issue.

Thus it was agreed that the parents must be called in for a meeting and informed about this. The teacher presented her case to the parents and told them that they must consult a doctor to get some help for dyspraxia. The family became angry and the next day the team were informed that Michael would not be back and had moved schools.

The team could not understand why this had happened and they were hurt by this response. The team at the new school did not make contact and it was never known how the issues were followed up.

- Do we know how Michael felt? Did the team? How do you know?
- How did the team inform their observations about Michael?
- How did the Welfare Assistant and the School Nurse feel? How do you know?
- How did the team feel when meeting the parents? How do you know?
- How did the parents feel?

Could you rewrite this whole scenario in an emotionally literate way?

Challenging assumptions

Without a doubt the team in the case study above had the best of intentions, but as we saw in the last chapter, making assumptions and labelling families and children is unhelpful. But it is so often done if a young child is not fitting into our 'expectations'. It is too common to hear teachers 'diagnose' children they work with and these labels can cause upset and high emotion.

As teachers, we hold a very responsible position and as such we are privileged to help shape the lives of the youngest children.

We need to be very careful about sensitive information, how it's used and interpreted. And how we share it with parents.

> Is 'emotional literacy' the same as 'emotional intelligence'?

Emotional literacy in daily provision and the curriculum

What is meant by the word 'curriculum'?

In practice, this is what decisions we make about what we teach, when we teach it, and how it will look in practice form our 'curriculum'. It is clear from previous chapters that before we take on our role a 'teacher' we must be clear about our own thinking and how we present ourselves.

Through working on our own emotional literacy it must automatically become our aim to enable the children to become emotionally literate too. This penultimate chapter looks at what needs to be considered to develop this, and Chapter Eight will sum this up by reflecting on practical planning.

We teachers must see ourselves as researchers, able to think, and to produce a true curriculum, a curriculum created from the needs of all individual children. However, what we so often do is impose adult time on children's time, and this inevitably negates children being able to work with their own resources.

This word does not always sit well with teachers of the youngest children, but it is important that we use it and define it appropriately. The Statutory Framework of each country defines the 'curriculum', or 'educational programmes' that we teach. So we are given the parameters within which we develop the teaching as appropriate for each cohort of children we work with. To do this effectively we need to be very clear what we understand by the words 'teaching' and 'learning'.

Chapter Six: How emotional literacy supports an inclusive environment

> Reflect on the words 'teaching' and 'learning'. What do they mean to you? How do you know when you are being an effective 'teacher'? How do you know when 'learning' has been effective?
>
> What do you remember about school? Write down a positive and a negative memory. What are your reasons for each choice?

My lasting memory of school is how it was drummed into me that I am not very good at maths. I wonder how many people reading this feel like that? I was once made to stand in front of the class to count the dinner money as it was put on the teacher's desk. I was ten, and this was before decimalisation. I can remember everything about that experience, and it was just one example of that teacher publicly making an example of my mathematical inadequacy. Unsurprisingly this has stuck with me. Whilst that is a long time ago, it is surprising how many practices still exist that make children feel inadequate. Often this is done unintentionally, but the effect is there.

> Use your reflections from the previous five chapters to think about effectively fostering emotional literacy. Remember to filter your thinking through:
>
> - Our core documents, both statutory and for guidance as they consistently remind us of this with references to personal, social and emotional development
> - Our own feelings and understandings as they will determine how we understand and interpret what we read.

My school experience actually informed my decision to become a teacher. The curriculum is not just what is taught, it is *how* it's taught. Our own understandings and feelings and how we interpret them are key here.

Pause here to reflect on what has an impact on how you go about your daily work, and the provision you make for the children. Consider the effects of:

- Expectations
- Personal feelings
- Assumptions
- Outside influences
- Other people.

As you do this, add to your list of words that describe emotions.

What is meant by the word 'provision'?

What we provide – the 'provision' – is ultimately defined by the adults and the effects of the points above. This is simply because they are in charge of the budgets and the maintenance of the venue. However, although many decisions have to be taken by the adults, the families and children must be part of the decision making in an emotionally literate environment.

All those involved, whether teachers, children or their parents and carers must be reflected in provision and curriculum decisions.

> **Remember...**
>
> Remember that you are a key resource within your provision. And sometimes you are the only constant factor in someone's life.
>
> 'The child *depends* on his toys. He *depends* on his environment'.

'We aren't little people, we are children'

I once visited a school where a child overheard me saying something to his teacher where I referred to the children as 'little people'. This little boy came up to me and said 'we aren't little people, we are children'. This was a pivotal moment for me. Being a child is important in its own right and must be recognised as such. This is the starting point for creating an emotionally literate provision and subsequently curriculum.

Chapter Seven: Emotional literacy in daily provision and the curriculum

> How do you refer to the children in your setting? How you refer to them is a reflection of how you think and feel about them. I once refused to have a supply teacher back in my Reception Class because she referred to the children as 'little maggots'. What are the children learning from you?

How we refer to the families, children and our colleagues is important. Look back at the vocabulary you listed in Chapter Five.

Think about...

> Make a list of all the current vocabulary that is used daily to describe children and families. For example 'hard to reach' or 'below age related expectations'. How does using this vocabulary affect how you see the children?

It is the responsibility of the Key Persons in the provision to make the curriculum and provision emotionally literate.

The hidden curriculum

In order to create an emotionally literate provision, the 'hidden curriculum' must be acknowledged and addressed. Remember the discussion in Chapter Four about how what we are feeling affects what we do?

> You never come in an isolated way; you always come with pieces of the world attached to you. So the meetings that we have are always contaminated with the experiences that we bring with us.
> (Your Image of the Child: Where Teaching Begins, by Loris Malaguzzi www.reggioalliance.org)

How we are also affects the way we develop what we provide. The children will notice everything and easily pick up messages. Whether they are intended or not.

Take an objective look at the environment you provide. If this is difficult, invite a trusted visitor in to give their opinion. It is a good idea to kneel down to view the environment - this will give you the child's eye view. This is where the 'teaching begins'. There is an audit in the Appendix to help you with this.

Reflect on the feeling below. Might your provision make a child feel like this?

How would you feel if you walked into an unfamiliar environment that was brightly coloured, full of things you didn't recognise or understand, every object was shiny and had different squiggles on?

You didn't know what anything meant and grown ups kept using words you didn't understand like 'line up here', 'tidy up time' and 'circle time'. Grown ups kept getting cross with you when you were playing with the trains. They made you stop and took you buy the hand to a table to look at more squiggles, this time on paper. They asked you questions that you didn't understand and didn't smile at you. The trains had been packed away out of your reach when the grown up had finished with you. You stood hopefully pointing at the box and saying please, but another grown up took your hand and said 'No, it's small group time now'.

What would you do? What messages are being given by your setting?

Chapter Seven: Emotional literacy in daily provision and the curriculum

What makes you feel comfortable? Uncomfortable? Is this an emotionally literate way of creating a curriculum?

It is crucial that the child feels secure and respected within relationships and interactions with the adults. Children learn how the world works through how we communicate and respond to them. This works in a negative way too – children will also very easily learn things from us that we do not want them to learn. For example:

- You get more attention if you behave inappropriately
- You get what you want if you are bigger and louder than others
- Sharing is about giving away something you are playing with
- Adults are always on someone else's side when things go wrong
- Adults are there to tell you off and stop you doing things
- You can hurt people and take things so long as you say sorry.

This list is not exclusive and you will be able to add more after you have reflected on your own environment. What sort of curriculum would you prefer to teach?

The negotiated classroom

Inevitably, we are responsible for the development of provision and the environment we create for the children. However this should not mean that we must make all the decisions. It important that the children are involved in how the environment develops and that the decisions made include them. This way of working is not always easy.

> The idea of learning being negotiated is a challenge to any curriculum which prescribes the process and content of experiences without taking into account the current needs and interests of children. (Fisher 1996)

This is because we are looking to provide a curriculum 'which starts from the child rather than expecting the child to start from the curriculum' (ibid). The children are enabled to have agency in the provision and the curriculum.

This type of negotiated environment describes what is needed in an emotionally literate environment. This sensitive style creates a balanced provision in which to learn.

In order to have a negotiated classroom, it is important to have secure rules and routines that are understood and make sense to everyone. If a situation is not understood, then there is potential for confusion and difficulties. This requires a consistency of approach on the part of the team, and also understanding the children and families (Chapters Four and Five).

The emotionally literate team will also understand:

> Children's feelings should also be respected. It is questionable whether adults should attempt to jolly children along when they are bereft at being left in the nursery, or when their friend will not play with them. (Dowling 2007)

Time to reflect:
As you reflect on your provision and the curriculum you offer, consider these points:

- **How do my feelings affect how I interact with individual children?**
- **How well have new children come to terms with their feelings when they start in our setting?**
- **What have I done today (this week) to help children be more aware of their feelings?**
- **How many routines and rules in the setting are totally in the interests of the children's wellbeing?**
- **How many rules and routines are for the convenience of the adults?**
- **How does our setting reflect a true partnership with families and children?**
- **How do you feel when they came into the setting?**
- **Does everyone know the environment and where everything is?**
- **How do we feel when we are told what to do and where to go in an unfamiliar situation?**
- **Do you feel as if no one is listening to you?**
- **How do you think the children feel?**

At this point stop to reflect: is 'emotional literacy' the same as 'emotional intelligence'? And how does understanding this impact provision, teaching and learning: the curriculum?

Chapter Seven: Emotional literacy in daily provision and the curriculum

> **Case study**
>
> A delegate on one of my courses once shared this story with the group. As you read: consider how it makes you feel and how it might apply to your daily practice.

> **Case study: The surprise**
>
> The couple had just celebrated a significant wedding anniversary and were going away for a long weekend as a treat leaving their two grown up children looking after their house. They didn't know that the children had a surprise planned for a special gift to be ready for when they got back.
>
> For a long time the Mum had been bothered by the state of her kitchen and was planning to have it modernised and decorated. The children planned to do the sorting and decorating themselves. As soon as their parents had left, they went shopping for all the materials they needed – they had established the sort of colour scheme their Mum wanted without her knowing their plans.
>
> Over the weekend all the furniture and fittings were removed from the kitchen and stacked in the living areas of the house and the decorating was started. However the children had underestimated the size of the task, and they were unable to finish and return all the fixtures and fittings before their parents came back. So the living areas were still being used as storage and the kitchen was not functional.
>
> On Monday evening the parents arrived home after a long journey. There had been problems on the motorway and the traffic was bad. They had been looking forward to resting in the familiar surroundings of home.
>
> But home did not look the same. What had been planned as a lovely surprise was actually very unsettling and upsetting. For everyone, but particularly for Mum as she knew that this was meant to make her happy and this was the opposite of what she was feeling.

> What might the grown up children have done differently? Now reflect on the alterations and changes you make in your provision when the children have gone home. How do you think the children feel when they arrive the next morning?

The delegate shared this personal experience during a session about wellbeing where we were examining 'transition' and change. She said that she still 'shudders' when she remembers what happened and how it had the opposite effect to that intended. She wasn't even sure that she would have been completely happy if the project had been finished when she got home. How does this story relate to including emotional literacy in our daily provision and curriculum? Compare it to this:

> **Case study: The home corner**
>
> The teachers had been watching the children playing and had seen that many were really interested in dinosaurs. When the children had all gone home, the adults set about turning the Home Corner into a dinosaur cave. They moved all the Home Corner equipment into the shed and spent hours replacing it with all sorts of other resources, including some they made themselves. A great deal of time was spent on this, and they were pleased with the results. They were also excited and looking forward to seeing the faces of the children in the morning.
>
> The next morning they watched and waited. A few children investigated the new 'cave', spent a few minutes there then wandered off. During the course of the morning the teachers began to notice that bits of Home Corner equipment were appearing back in the environment. The shed was always open for children to select their own equipment, so the children had got out most of the resources that had only just been put away and set up another Home Corner, placing it neatly in the Reading Corner.
>
> The Dinosaur Cave was largely ignored, but the children continued their interest in dinosaurs. And their version of the Home Corner stayed in place.

Chapter Seven: Emotional literacy in daily provision and the curriculum

> What similarities and differences did you notice in these two studies? How often have you had a similar experience to the team in the second study? Why did it happen?

Conclusion

Creating an emotionally literate provision to underpin an appropriate curriculum requires us to analyse everything we do to consider how it affects everyone involved. The list below is of common practice seen in provision, that can have a negative impact on the children, and the families. Can you see why?

- Differentiation and grouping
- Group names
- Walls covered with laminated prints
- Displays made from adult pictures decorated by the children
- Areas set up in a specific way with specific resources
- Displays of 'targets' and how close children are to reaching them
- Environments that are changed to meet the themes decided by the adults
- Behaviour charts
- Pictures showing perceived 'right' and 'wrong' ways of holding pencils
- Daily timetables that dictate regular changes and different environments.

Alexander (2004) writes:

> In the alternative pedagogy, the teacher engages, as a matter of necessity, with a number of distinct but related domains of ideas and values. Firstly, and most immediately, these are concerned with:
>
> - children: their characteristics, development and upbringing;
> - learning: how it can best be motivated, achieved, identified, assessed and built upon;
> - teaching: its planning, execution and evaluation; and
> - curriculum: the various ways of knowing, understanding, doing, creating, investigating and making sense which it is desirable for children to encounter, and how these are most appropriately translated and structured for teaching.

It is vital that we do appropriately translate and structure our teaching and learning environments so that they start with the child, thus making our provision emotionally literate. The list above is full of ideas that do not do this. Robin Alexander goes on to say:

> Clearly, pedagogy is a somewhat more complex enterprise than may be recognised by those who reduce effective teaching to 'what works', or 'best practice' lessons downloaded from government websites. (Alexander 2004)

This is an important statement to bear in mind as you start to work through Chapter Eight, the final chapter.

Emotional Literacy in the early years

Fostering emotional literacy in the setting

...the teacher's task is first to nourish and assist, to watch, encourage, guide, induce, rather than to interfere, prescribe, or restrict.
(Montessori – The Montessori Method)

Every child is 'a unique child'

The problem that we have in the current age is that we have access to so many curriculum ideas and packages. A quick search using the terms 'emotional' and 'Early Years' on the internet reveals so many products that can be bought, downloaded or trained up on. These all aim to enable you to support children with understanding their emotions, and describing their feelings. So often these products dazzle, but they do not actually illuminate in that they can direct the child to label themselves to satisfy the teacher. For example, by sticking a picture of how they 'feel' on a board when they arrive in the morning the child has 'told' the teacher something. This then stays there for the rest of the day, and the adults feel that they have 'ticked a box'. But what is actually learnt here? Everyone has played their part and the daily routine is completed as a dazzling visual, but what has actually been illuminated?

Return to your thinking on this - Is 'emotional literacy' the same as 'emotional intelligence'?

In this final chapter, we will draw together the threads from the book in order to consolidate thinking and move forward.

Time for reflection

At the beginning of Chapter One I outlined two statements as useful lenses through which to review your reading. Everything in this book has used these 'lenses' as a root.

Chapter Seven: Emotional literacy in daily provision and the curriculum

They are:

- Our core documents, both statutory and for guidance as they consistently remind us of this with references to personal, social and emotional development
- Our own feelings and understandings as they will determine how we understand and interpret what we read.

Alongside keeping these in mind, was the task to start making a list of all the words you notice related to emotions, feelings, or well being. All the while adding to this list and reflecting on each word noted.

It is the second of the two 'lenses' that is the more important to be clear about.

This is the one that will most inform our work and how we are towards all those around us. And how they are towards us.

This is my reflection on a conference I once went to.

> Throughout the day the subject of behaviour charts was a recurring theme. This was because a recent television programme had depicted children starting school in Reception class and the use of a 'sun and rain cloud' type of behaviour chart. The use of this involves children having their names moved from the sun to the cloud if they have behaved in a way that is not deemed appropriate by the teacher. In the instance depicted during the programme, a little boy was deemed not to have been listening. This resulted in his name being moved onto the cloud and him looking upset. He was also asked to sit against the wall to the side of the room.
>
> A delegate in the audience shared that when her little girl had visited her new Reception class the summer before she was due to start, the teacher spent time talking to children about their new environment and what they could expect when they started. One of these 'expectations' was around behaviour and the type of chart mentioned above was shown and explained. The little girl spent the summer break before she started her new class terrified of not 'behaving' and being moved onto the 'rain cloud'. So when she finally started in September she was very unsettled.

Think about...

Compare this account to the story about the key in Chapter One. Does this evoke the same feelings? How would you describe the feelings in this scenario for:

- **The child**
- **The parent**
- **The teacher**
- **The conference delegates**.

There are some fundamental understandings missing here. It is important to recognise these before we move into thinking about how we might plan for 'emotional literacy'.

Is 'emotional literacy' the same as 'emotional intelligence'?

The terms are used interchangeably, but are actually quite different. This is key to fundamental

Chapter Eight: Planning and activities to foster emotional literacy

understanding of emotion. In the example in Chapter One, specifically the example of the 'key' being left at nursery so Mum would have to come back, and the example of the behaviour chart above, the teachers are demonstrating 'emotional intelligence'. This is because they have been given knowledge of a technique to use and which they are implementing. However, what is missing here is 'emotional literacy' because that technique has not been researched, unpicked, considered, reflected upon and, most of all, has not been viewed through the lens of:

- Our own feelings and understandings as they will determine how we understand and interpret what we read.

Of course, our own feelings and understandings are coloured and affected by our own experiences as children. This must be taken into account and addressed.

It is not good enough just to say that having your name on the 'rain cloud of the behaviour chart' never did you any harm, and therefore making it right to use the rain cloud chart in your practice. This may well be 'emotional intelligence', but it is not emotionally 'literate'.

Paul Dix (2017) writes about something that he calls 'emotional currency':

> Great teachers build emotional currency with their pupils deliberately. They know that there will be a time when it can be spent – a crisis averted, an angry acceleration halted. (Dix 2017)

He notes that things and actions such as 'the kind word, the offer of help, the compassion in times of trouble' are the skills that we can so easily use in those opportunities that often present themselves. And that we should not give up too quickly as it can often take months to break through the barriers with the 'drip effect' of kindnesses.

> With a pile of emotional currency in the bank you can afford to give the child opportunities to take risks, knowing that you can support them if they fail. Done well, the drip effect of positive recognition beats grand material rewards that shine brightly but soon. (Dix 2017)

Remember...

You are the Key Person and it is for you to make sure that every child's experience is emotionally stable and consistent. This means creating a culture of mutual trust and respect. Why is this culture key to underpinning Practical Planning and Activities? Have you considered how the 'culture' that you bring with you, will not be the same as the 'culture' that the families and children bring with them?

Consider your response to this question before you carry on reading.

By now you will have created a fairly long list of words and phrases that are examples of emotions and feelings. If you have been working on this book as team it's worth comparing lists to look for similarities and differences.

Whatever you find in your comparisons, I imagine that everyone will have 'happy', 'sad' 'angry' and 'afraid' somewhere on their list. These emotions are usually at the core of any planning or activity that is prepared with a view to enabling the youngest children to express themselves. Having worked through this book it will have become clear that this is quite a simplistic viewpoint and that 'emotional literacy' is far more nuanced. This means that we must be very careful and clear what we are planning and why. This requires us to have a principled approach.

Before we move on to what we might plan to foster emotional literacy, we need to be clear what is meant by 'activities'.

What is an 'activity'?

The word 'activity' is one that is so often used without thinking. What does it mean to you? What do you understand by 'planning' and 'activities'?

I find that asking practitioners why something is planned or happening in their settings can lead to confused responses or answers based on the idea that 'we always do it' or it has not really been thought about. If we are to be truly emotionally literate teachers then we need to be very careful to avoid this response. We are moving into an era where policy dictates so much of what we do, so it is vital that we

Chapter Eight: Planning and activities to foster emotional literacy

review everything we do through the two lenses at the start of every chapter. And that we now add a third:

- How am I enabling the children in my care to look after their own mental health?

Of course it is important that we understand our feelings and the impact that we make with them. This last chapter will develop that to explore how we make an impact on the children we work with.

> Take a look at your setting and ask yourself:
>
> - How many children do you see across a week?
> - What is the age range?
> - How much time are children in your setting?
> - How many practitioners do you have in total?
> - How often do you interact with the families and involve them in what you do?
> - What do you actually know about the backgrounds, cultures and beliefs of all those that you work with? Adults and children alike - including the families.

Why are these questions important? In any given setting there could be a huge diversity of backgrounds, cultures and beliefs each new child across the threshold could bring something new or just a little different – note the numbers of possibilities given above.

The questions above are important to inform us so that we can 'read' situations and work appropriately with all with whom we come into contact. We need to reflect on:

- What do the children understand about their world and different events in it?
- Are they secure within the setting?
- Do they understand that everyone has a different background and a different point of view?
- In fact do the children have a 'sense of self'?
- Are they developmentally ready for what we are expecting?
- Is what we are expecting appropriate for all involved?

I once visited a nursery where I saw children not yet two years old sitting in high chairs with green paint to colour in a pre-printed picture of a shamrock for St Patrick's Day.

The whole group was expected to complete one of these pictures. As each child finished they were lifted out of the chair, put back on the ground and another was picked up and put in their place. The wet paintings were put on the drying rack.

At the end of the day, the paintings were still there and the children had gone home without them. The next day they were thrown away to make space for new work.

> **Think about...**
>
> Reflect on what has happened in this case study. Does this activity foster 'emotional literacy'?

A pedagogical approach

In order to adopt an emotionally literate pedagogical approach to how provision and the environment are appropriately developed, it is useful to use a '**what, why, how**' approach to question everything that we think might be a good idea. For example:

- **What have we decided to do?**
- **Why is it important to do this?**
- **How will it affect the children/ the teachers/ the families?**
- **How will this be appropriate for the developmental stages of the children?**
- **How will further our thinking on emotional literacy?**

The questions will not always be the same, but it is important that everyone is clear about how the provision and the environment will impact on all.

'Happy', 'Sad' 'Angry' and 'Afraid'

The four basic emotions are a good starting point in discussing emotions, and there are many products and 'programmes' that encourage this. Before investing in any of these use the three questions approach – 'what, why and how?' - to see how useful the product will actually be. During the course of this book it has often been noted that emotions can be displayed in a variety of ways

Chapter Eight: Planning and activities to foster emotional literacy

in reaction to a variety of things. We all read situations differently, and a lack of emotional literacy on the part of the teachers can be a trigger.

> When practitioners understand the crucial role of sensitive periods in facilitating early brain development, they can think more critically about their planning of the environment and what changes can be made to maximise each child's learning experience. (Conkbayir, 2017)

Think about...

What do you understand by the 'sensitive periods' in early brain development? This is an important part of follow up reading.

Contributions from others

This section consists of pieces that have been written for me by friends and colleagues as I have been gathering thinking for this book. Everything they have shared can be applied to any setting, any age group and any adult.

As you read each study, reflect on your own practice and provision. Are there similarities to your practice? Differences? What would work for you? What wouldn't work? Why not?

When you have read these contributions use your thinking to write a summary of your own practice.

Chloe's Experiences
In the day nursery

I began working in my setting as part of my college work experience. Straight away I felt very welcomed and could tell that the setting tried hard to make me feel as part of the team. Through feeling welcome and the support that was provided, I was able to increase my confidence and become the best practitioner that I could become. I joined the team as a full-time member and worked alongside the manager and staff in order to provide the best care for the children attending the nursery. We ensure to provide a positive, nurturing environment to support the children's development as well as providing support for parents and carers. We work forward to promote an emotionally positive setting that the children can thrive in.

Chapter Eight: Planning and activities to foster emotional literacy

Beth's Experiences

Cuddles for settling in

I worked in a day nursery where there was a lot of traffic coming through the room on a regular basis – toddlers going into the garden, staff going to other areas of the nursery. One little boy had not long started in our preschool section and he came to sit on my lap for a while. Knowing that he was fairly new and would need some warmth and affection to help him settle, I let him sit on my lap for as long as he needed, while encouraging him to engage in an activity at the table next to us. A senior member of the team walked through at one point and said, 'Don't let him stay there too long', as though I was doing something wrong. I felt like I wanted to respond immediately with all the reasons why it was important that I let him stay on my lap as long as he needed - but it would have been inappropriate to do that in front of him, so I had to wait until later to give feedback away from the children.

Handover time

As a childminder, I had all the time I needed to talk to parents when they arrived at the beginning and end of their children's sessions. I would invite them in and we could have extensive conversations with their child about their day, showing them all the lovely things they had been doing and looking at their photographs. In stark contrast to this, in a pack-away preschool setting where all of the children arrived and departed at once, it was very difficult to have even one conversation, let alone speak with all of the parents. In this setting, it was only when children had struggled that we took parents to one side to chat about their day. I sometimes gave children a sticker saying things like, 'ask me about… the tower I built today' which would prompt conversation with their families later.

Teamwork and respect

When I worked in a community preschool there were members of staff who had been working there for anything up to sixteen years. Some of the staff were great and seemed to really enjoy their job, interacting well with the children and keeping the energy up. Others were not so enthusiastic and often complained about having to put out the tables and chairs for lunch time or change what was on display boards. It was challenging to work in this kind of environment because when others were not enthusiastic, it was easy to lack respect for them. However, when working with children, I knew how important it was that we model respect amongst the adults to show children how to respect one another. This would help the children to build their emotional literacy in terms of their relationships with adults and their peers.

How we provide an emotionally literate environment – The Playgroup

1. We acknowledge the child's perspective and empathise with the child- we let the child vent out their emotions- then they are ready to move on. We treat each child individually and with respect. They start forming a special relationship with someone outside their family. Feeling understood brings a soothing effect on their whole perspective and behaviour.

2. Let's talk together strategies of wait watch and listen helped us to understand the children well. it actually gave the children the power to express themselves. All expressions may not be in words but expressions are listened with care and empathy. approving their emotions and accepting them as they make them more comfortable. Our acceptance teaches the child that their emotions are not dangerous or shameful but are universal and manageable.

3. Children express their feelings, but they also learn from here how to shift gears to find constructive solutions to problems. That takes practice and modelling on our part.

4. provide with an opportunity to help children "play" out his big inner conflicts and let him resolve them so he can move on to the next age-appropriate developmental challenge.

I think all these works together for us and the team has learned the skills through experience and trainings.

Chapter Eight: Planning and activities to foster emotional literacy

Katherine's Experiences as the Day Nursery Manager
Respect

We treat everyone as we wish to be treated ourselves. Our motto is 'do as you would be done by'. I would never ask anyone to do anything that I wouldn't do myself. I believe in respect – look after people and they will look after you.

We encourage our children to be independent, outgoing and confident. Names are important and all the children know each other's names. There is always a happy buzz of conversation and the adults are always at the child's eye level to engage in conversation. We don't jump in too soon, we read the situation and then interact, offer help or join in.

Ed Vainker, Executive Principal & Director, Reach Children's Hub
The Principal's Vision

We have invested significantly in making sure that our staff are attachment aware. For us that means making sure that they understand the importance of a child's attachment but, crucially, also that they recognise their own capacity to have a profoundly positive influence on a child's attachment. Our staff are aware that by building strong relationships with children they can have a reparative impact on our most vulnerable children.

We also start from the assumption that behaviour is communication and seek to be curious about what a child might be trying to tell us in the way they are behaving. It is often very helpful for staff to do a home visit if a pupil is struggling and we have often found that something foundation like insufficient sleep, the absence of a parent or struggles with eating have been at the root of a period of a change in behaviour.

Finally, we believe that modelling is important. The more that our leaders are warm and kind, the easier and more likely it is that our front-line staff are treating our pupils in the same way.

Tony Ulatowski
Using Body, Mind and Breathe to support Emotional Literacy

High emotions and energy can be like the accelerator of a car that is stuck. It is stuck on not fully on but it is stuck, racing, and this is like stress to the nervous system. To the sympathetic system this is the fight or flight system so it is always on high alert. What we need to do with these young children is to teach them how to handle that and how to regulate their emotions along with their actions. By teaching them different types of breathing techniques they begin to feel and sense when they are feeling anger or high anxiety from the pressure of their environment in the classroom or anywhere else for that matter. The children start to learn what it feels like and how to change their emotions. They learn through physical movement in conjunction with breathing that they are actively doing something that is constructive and is physical movement with calming breathing. In this way we start to stimulate the parasympathetic nervous system, the calming system, the system that caresses mental awareness. This is the system that helps to calm the brainstem and the limbic system, the emotional centre of the brain.

By slowing down breathing with a physical movement, children begin to understand that it makes them feel good, being in control of themselves instead of running off, wild and random, tantrums or anger or worse physical violence. Children begin to learn how to self-regulate. This is a good thing for them and it makes them feel alive because they're in control therefore they start to feel included into other activities. When they are included they know they can take control and interact without judgement, actively communicating within their classroom and social communities.

Conclusion

The importance of understanding, and demonstrating, emotional literacy cannot be underestimated. The aim of this book has been to enable team reflection and professional development. This will not have always been easy as it will require some self-reflection and honesty, but we owe this to the children, families and colleagues we work with.

Appendices

An audit of provision

This is based on the quote used in Chapter Four. It is not to be seen as recommending a Reggio Emilia approach, but rather to be used as a useful focus when reviewing the emotionally literate environment.

Review	Discussion
The environment you construct around you and the children	
How does this reflect the image you have about the child?	
Is the environment that you are able to build based on a preconceived image of the child?	
Is the environment that you can build based on the child you see in front of you?	
Is the environment that grows out of your relationship with the child unique and fluid?	
How does the quality and quantity of relationships among you as adults and educators reflect your image of the child?	
What can the children see and sense of the spirit of what is going on among the adults in their world?	
Do the children understand whether the adults are working together in a truly collaborative way?	
Do staff show that they work in cooperation, or are they separated in some way from each other, living their experience as if it were private with little interaction?	

(Your Image of the Child: Where Teaching Begins, by Loris Malaguzzi www.reggioalliance.org

Appendices

What could we do instead?

Before changing anything in practice or provision you will be asking the 'what, why, how' questions. By now you will have started to reflect on different types of practice – yours and that of others. In the spirit of Paul Dix, that nothing changes until the adults change. Below are some ideas to prompt discussion about how things could be done differently in your setting. These are just suggestions, that you may not choose to use. There is space to add your own.

> Developmentally appropriate practices result from the process of professionals making decisions about the well-being and education of children based on at least three important kinds of information or knowledge:
>
> 1. what is known about child development and learning
> 2. what is known about the strengths, interests, and needs of each individual child in the group to be able to adapt for and be responsive to inevitable individual variation; and
> 3. knowledge of the social and cultural contexts in which children live to ensure that learning experiences are meaningful, relevant, and respectful for the participating children and their families.
>
> (www.naeyc.org)

What we do now	Emotionally Literate? Yes/No Give reasons	What could we do instead?
Set daily written tasks with theme given	No. Not respectful of individual ideas	Helicopter stories Story scribing
Set daily challenges	No. Not taking into account individual needs and interests	Sustained shared thinking
Decide themes and topics	No. As above. Also potentially disrespectful of 'cultural capital'	'We aren't little people, we're children' Children have agency
Environment is set up daily	No. As above	Children have free access to resources
Decisions are made about the environment	No. As above. Also not respectful of the security that many young children require in a consistent environment	Children share in the decisions giving them ownership
Behaviour charts	No. Labels children and certain behaviours as problematic without taking time to understand reasons and support the child	Provide a supportive environment where children feel their wellbeing is cared about and they are able to understand expectations that make sense to them
Ability grouping	No. Again children are labelled and learning is easily 'capped' as assumptions are made of capability	Observations are used sensitively to really get to know the children and develop their individual skills and knowledge through well informed provision
Laminated notices on various surfaces inside and outside	No. Much of what is displayed makes no sense to the children and does not relate to anything that is familiar them. The environment is intimidating to them?	Make sure that any labels and notices used throughout the environment are relevant, authentic and reflect real life

Remember the entries above are just some rough ideas to get you started. You do not have to use them.

Appendices

Provision and environment audit

Use these questions to collect evidence of practice, inform staff at meetings and support action plans.

The Emotional Environment
How do my daily routines make it possible for me to get to know and treat each child as an individual?
How does my environment demonstrate to children that they are welcome?
How well have new children come to terms with their feelings on admission? How do I know?
Do we have a partnership with parents that is truly two-way?
How do the staff interact with each other?
Do your staff make time to talk with parents and carers – do the children see their parents sharing friendly conversation and laughter with their practitioners?
Are the children happy when they arrive and when they leave?
What have I done today (this week) to help children be more aware of their feelings?
Do we respect the feelings of the children?
Do we respect the feelings of the families?
How do my feelings affect how I interact with individuals?
How do I interact with children? Do I get down at their level and give them a chance to express themselves?
Are the skills of conversation modelled?
Do children lead interactions?
Is open-ended questioning used?
Are children engaged in their play – can they approach an adult for support when necessary?
Does planning reflect the needs of the children?
How are the children able to be independent? To make decisions and choices?
How does the environment encourage this?
Are the resources of good quality and do children value them?
Does the routine allow children time to follow through their ideas?
Are the children involved in how the environment is set out?
What can be seen that is child initiated?
How does my room arrangement encourage children to talk together, share and co-operate?
Is children's own work proudly displayed, or has it been adapted by the adults to 'neaten' it up?
Are the displays at a height where the children can see them and become engaged with them?
Is there only work by the adults on display? Why is this?
Is everything clean and well cared for?
How out of date are displays? Does anyone notice them anymore?

Appendices

Reflections on Emotional Literacy

Discussion	
Personal	Professional

Appendices

The Emotional Health Lead

Many settings now have an Emotional Health Lead. This is an important role, that needs careful thought, preparation and training. It is also a role that will require time to be executed effectively, and the support of the rest of the team.

If you have, or are planning to have, an Emotional Health Lead at your setting it is important to have a clear understanding of what the role will look like and involve.

An important reference text for giving more details about the role is 'Leading on Pastoral Care' by Daniel Sobel (see References). I have drawn the points on the table below from this book as a starting point to define the role and responsibilities of this key job.

Teaching	Teaching
What do you understand by the role?	
What does the team understand by the role?	
What do the families understand about the role?	
What does the team understand by 'behaviour'?	
What is included in the role of Emotional Health Lead?	
What policies are in place that support the role of Emotional Health Lead?	
Is there a consistent understanding of how the team works with families?	
How is the self-esteem of individuals supported?	
How are transitions understood and supported?	
How are the team supported to cope with challenges?	
What is done really well to support good emotional health at the setting?	
What could be improved?	
How well do we communicate?	
How does the paperwork we already complete support emotional literacy for the team?	
How does the paperwork we already complete support emotional literacy for families and children?	
How does the physical environment exemplify and underpin a team understanding emotional literacy?	

Appendices

Key vocabulary of emotions

This list is not exhaustive, and throughout your reflections on the case studies in this book, you will come up with your own.

Happy	Like	Positive	Respectful
Sad	Dislike	Negative	Disrespectful
Calm	Confused	Keen	Bored
Angry	Confident	Satisfied	Teaching
Nervous	Wary	Dissatisfied	Learning
Anxious	Unsettled	Pressured	Deflated
Stressed	Settled	Relaxed	Optimistic
Cross	Sure	Frustrated	Useless
Preoccupied	Unsure	Tense	Inadequate
Bothered	Distressed	Defensive	Capable
Shy	Wobbly	Offensive	High achieving
Lonely	Sick	Tantrums	Less able
Scared	Panicky	Distaste	More able
Afraid	Wary	Sulky	Humiliated
Depressed	Freaked out	Provoking	Concern
Upset	'like a fish in water'	Rude	Interest
Worried	Empathy	Compliant	Worry
Terrified	Sympathy	Disagreeable	Understand
Insecure	Tentative	Confident	Care
Excited	Revolted	Self assured	Need

> How would you know that a child, or an adult, was feeling any of these emotions? Would everyone display the same signs? What might you notice? How do you know when you are feeling any kind of emotion? How useful, or appropriate, is it to label feelings and emotions?

Notes

References

Alexander, R. (2004) Still no pedagogy? Principle, pragmatism and compliance in primary education. University of Cambridge, Cambridge Journal of Education, Vol. 34, No. 1, March 2004

Brooker L. (2002) Starting School – Young Children Learning Cultures. Buckingham. Open University Press

Brooker, L (2008) Supporting Transitions in the Early Years Maidenhead. Open University Press

Conkbayir, M. (2017). Early Childhood and Neuroscience. Theory, Research and Implications for Practice. London: Bloomsbury Academic

Chugani, H.T et al (1998) Local Brain Functional Activity Following Early Deprivation: A Study of Post-institutionalised Romanian Orphans. Neuroimage 14 (6)

Curriculum for Wales (Revised 2015) Foundation Phase Framework

Csikszentmihayli, M. (1979). The concept of flow. In: B. Sutton-Smith, Play and learning (pp. 257-273). New York, Gardner.

Department for Education (Northern Ireland 2013) Learning to Learn - A Framework for Early Years Education and Learning

Department for Education (2017) Statutory Framework for the Early Years Foundation Stage

Dix, P. (2017) When the Adults Change Everything Changes. Carmarthen. Independent Thinking Press

Fisher, J. (1996) Starting from the Child? Buckingham. Open University Press

Fisher, J. 2016 Interacting or Interfering? Maidenhead. Open University Press

Gerhardt, S. (2015) Why Love Matters. Hove. Routledge

Goddard-Blythe, S. (2005). The Well Balanced Child. Stroud: Hawthorn Press

Isaacs, S. (First printed 1937 This edition 2013) The Educational Value of the Nursery School. Copyright 2013 The British Association for Early Childhood Education

Laevers, F. (Ed.) in collaboration with: Mieke Daems, Griet De Bruyckere, Bart Declercq, Julia Moons, Kristien Silkens, Gerlinde Snoeck, Monique Van Kessel Well-being and Involvement in Care Settings. A Process-oriented Self-evaluation Instrument. © 2005 Kind & Gezin and Research Centre for Experientel Education

Laevers, F. (2015) Making care and education more effective through wellbeing and involvement. An introduction to Experiential Education. Center for Experiential Education

Learning and Teaching Scotland, 2010 Pre-Birth to Three Positive Outcomes for Scotland's Children and Families Learning and Teaching Scotland National Guidance

Malaguzzi, L. Your Image of the Child: Where Teaching Begins www.reggioalliance.org

National Strategy Guidance: the key person in reception classes and small nursery settings Julian Grenier, Peter Elfer, Julia Manning Morton, Dilys Wilson and Katie Dearnley

O'Connor A. (2014) Understanding Transitions in the Early Years. Abingdon. Routledge

Reddy, V. (2008) How Infants Know Minds. USA. First Harvard University Press

Social and emotional wellbeing: early years Public health Guideline Published: 24 October 2012 nice.org.uk/guidance/ph40

Sobel, D (2019) Leading on Pastoral Care. London. Bloomsbury

Sroufe, L.A. (1997) Emotional Development: The Organisation of Emotional Life in the Early Years. Cambridge. Cambridge University Press

The Scottish Government, Edinburgh 2008 The Early Years Framework

www.naeyc.org Developmentally Appropriate Practice in Early Childhood Programs Serving Children from Birth through Age 8 Adopted 2009

Acknowledgements

The author would like to thank the following for their contributions:

Beth Thomas – for support and for sharing her experiences
Tony Ulatowski – for his wise words and conversations
Sonali and Beavers Preschool Hounslow
Katherine and Chiswick Toddlers World
Chloe – Key Person at Chiswick Toddlers World
Ed Vainker – Executive Principal & Director of Reach Children's Hub.